Collins
gem

P9-CJQ-477

FRENCH
PHRASEBOOK
& DICTIONARY

Published by Collins
An imprint of HarperCollins Publishers
Westerhill Road
Bishopbriggs
Glasgow G64 2QT

Fourth Edition 2016

10 9 8 7 6 5 4 3 2

© HarperCollins Publishers 1993, 2007, 2010, 2016

ISBN 978-0-00-813588-1

Collins® and Collins Gem® are registered trademarks of HarperCollins Publishers Limited

www.collinsdictionary.com

Typeset by Davidson Publishing Solutions, Glasgow

Printed and bound in China by RR Donnelley APS

A catalogue record for this book is available from the British Library.

If you would like to comment on any aspect of this book, please contact us at the given address or online.

E-mail: dictionaries@harpercollins.co.uk
 facebook.com/collinsdictionary
 @collinsdict

Acknowledgements
We would like to thank those authors and publishers who kindly gave permission for copyright material to be used in the Collins Corpus. We would also like to thank Times Newspapers Ltd for providing valuable data.

Editor
Holly Tarbet

Contributors
Marie Ollivier-Caudray
Anna Stevenson
David White

For the Publisher
Gerry Breslin
Janice McNeillie
Helen Newstead

Front cover image: Louvre museum in Paris. ©Elnur / Shutterstock.com

Using your phrasebook

Whether you're on holiday or on business, your **Collins Gem Phrasebook and Dictionary** is designed to help you locate the exact phrase you need, when you need it. You'll also gain the confidence to go beyond what is in the book, as you can adapt the phrases by using the dictionary section to substitute your own words.

The Gem Phrasebook and Dictionary includes:

• Over 60 topics arranged thematically, so that you can easily find an expression to suit the situation

• Simple pronunciation which accompanies each word and phrase, to make sure you are understood when speaking aloud

• Tips to safeguard against any cultural faux pas, providing the essential dos and don'ts of local customs or etiquette

• A basic grammar section which will help you to build on your phrases

• **FACE TO FACE** dialogue sections to give you a flavour of what to expect from a real conversation

• A handy map of the country which shows the major cities and how to pronounce them

• **YOU MAY HEAR** sections for common announcements and messages, so that you don't miss important information when out and about

- A user-friendly 3000 word dictionary to ensure you'll never be stuck for something to say

- **LIFELINE** phrases are listed on the inside covers for quick reference. These basic words and phrases will be essential to your time abroad

Before you jet off, it's worth spending time looking through the topics to see what is covered and becoming familiar with pronunciation.

The colour key below shows you how to search the phrasebook by theme, so you'll be able to find relevant phrases very quickly.

Talking to people
Getting around
Staying somewhere
Shopping
Leisure
Communications
Practicalities
Health
Eating out
Menu reader
Reference
Grammar
Dictionary

Contents

Pronouncing French

• •

In this book we have used a simple system to help you pronounce the phrases. We have designed the book so that as you read the pronunciation of the phrases you can follow the French. This will help you to recognize the different sounds and enable you to read French without relying on the guide. Here are a few rules you should know:

French	sounds like	example	pronunciation
au	oh	**autobus**	oh-toh-bews
c (+ a, o, u)	ka, ko, ku	**cas, col, cure**	ka, kol, kewr
c (+ e, i), ç	s	**ceci, ça**	suh-see, sa
ch	sh	**chat**	sha
é	ay	**été**	aytay
è	eh	**très**	treh
eau	oh	**beau**	boh
eu	uh	**neuf**	nuhf
g (+ e, i)	zhe, zhee	**gel, gîte**	zhel, zheet
gn	ny	**agneau**	a-nyoh
oi	wa	**roi**	rwa
u	ew	**sur**	sewr
ui	wee	**huit**	weet

e is sometimes weak and sounds like uh. This happens either in very short words (**je** zhuh, **le** luh, **se** suh, etc.) or when the **e** falls at the end of a syllable: **retard** ruh-tar, **depuis** duh-pwee.

h is not pronounced: **hôtel** oh-tel, **haricot** a-ree-koh.

There are nasal vowels in French (represented by ñ):

un uñ
fin/bain fañ/bañ
on oñ
dans/en dahñ/ahñ

Word endings are often silent: **Paris** pa-ree, **Londres** loñdr, **parlent** parl. However, the ending is sometimes pronounced if it is followed by a word which begins with a vowel:

avez-vous a-vay voo **but vous avez** voo za-vay.

In French, unlike English, there is normally no strong accent on any syllable, but instead a slight emphasis on the final syllable of each word, phrase and sentence, which takes the form of a rising intonation rather than an increase in volume.

Top ten tips

• • • • • • • • • • • • • • • • • • • •

1 Use **vous** instead of **tu** until you are asked to use
   the familiar form. Do not use first names until you
   are invited.

2 If you visit French people at their home, your
   hosts will appreciate a small gift of something
   typically British, such as tea, jam or biscuits.

3 Do not forget to stamp your train ticket before
   getting on the train – otherwise it will not be valid.

4 By law, French people must carry their ID cards all
   the time, and there could be ID inspections in the
   street (especially in big cities). The police will ask
   'Vos papiers, s'il vous plaît'.

5 If giving someone flowers, you should avoid
   chrysanthemums (they are funeral flowers) and
   red roses (they have romantic connotations).

6 Keep your hands on the table at all times during
   a meal – do not place them on your lap. Elbows,
   however, should be kept off the table!

7 If you are travelling by car in France, you should
   always be aware not to leave valuables in plain
   sight when parking in tourist sites and villages.

8 When addressing a stranger, always add **Monsieur** or **Madame**, even if you are only asking for directions.

9 In some areas (especially the countryside) people do not speak a word of English, so have your phrasebook ready!

10 If you are travelling and have a medical issue, you can call **SOS Médecins** (dial 3624). They will come to your hotel or home at any time, 24/7. You will usually be charged around 50–70 euros for this service.

Talking to people

Hello/goodbye, yes/no

You will find the French quite formal in their greetings, shaking hands both on meeting and on parting. French people, when they know each other well, greet each other with a kiss on each cheek. **Bonjour, madame** or **bonjour, monsieur** are the politest ways to greet someone. **Mademoiselle** is becoming less frequently used. **Salut** is more informal than **bonjour**. If someone offers you something, perhaps an extra serving of food, and you simply reply **merci**, they will take this to mean 'no'. You must say **oui, merci** or you will go hungry!

Please	**S'il vous plaît** seel voo pleh
Thanks (very much)	**Merci (beaucoup)** mehr-see (boh-koo)
You're welcome!	**De rien!** duh ryañ!
Yes	**Oui** wee
No	**Non** noñ

Yes, please	**Oui, merci**	
	wee, mehr-see	
No, thanks	**Non, merci**	
	noñ, mehr-see	
OK!	**D'accord!**	
	da-kor!	
Sir/Mr	**Monsieur/M.**	
	muh-syuh	
Madam/Mrs/Ms	**Madame/Mme**	
	ma-dam	
Miss	**Mademoiselle/Mlle**	
	mad-mwa-zel	
Hello/Hi	**Bonjour/Salut**	
	boñ-zhoor/sa-lew	
Goodbye/Bye	**Au revoir/Salut**	
	oh ruh-vwar/sa-lew	
Bye for now	**À bientôt**	
	a byañ-toh	
Good evening	**Bonsoir**	
	boñ-swar	
Goodnight	**Bonne nuit**	
	bon nwee	
See you tomorrow	**À demain**	
	a duh-mañ	
Excuse me! (to catch attention)	**Pardon, monsieur/madame!**	
	par-doñ, muh-syuh/ma-dam!	
Sorry!	**Pardon!**	
	par-doñ!	

| I'm sorry | **Je suis désolé(e)** |
| | zhuh swee day-zo-lay |

| How are you? | **Comment allez-vous?** |
| | ko-mahñ ta-lay voo? |

| Fine, thanks | **Très bien, merci** |
| | treh byañ, mehr-see |

| And you? | **Et vous?** |
| | ay voo? |

| I don't understand | **Je ne comprends pas** |
| | zhuh nuh koñ-prahñ pa |

| I speak very little French | **Je parle très peu le français** |
| | zhuh parl treh puh luh frahñ-seh |

Key phrases

• •

You don't need to say complicated things to get what you want. Often simply naming the thing and adding **s'il vous plaît** will do the trick, even when asking for directions.

| the (masculine) | **le** |
| | luh |

| (feminine) | **la** |
| | la |

| (plural) | **les** |
| | lay |

| the museum | **le musée** |
| | luh mew-zay |

the station	**la gare**
	la gar
the shops	**les magasins**
	lay ma-ga-zañ
a/one (masculine)	**un**
	uñ
(feminine)	**une**
	ewn
a ticket/	**un billet/un timbre**
one stamp	uñ bee-yeh/uñ tañbr
a room/	**une chambre/une bouteille**
one bottle	ewn shahñbr/ewn boo-tay-yuh
some (masculine)	**du**
	dew
(feminine)	**de la**
	duh la
(plural)	**des**
	day
some wine	**du vin**
	dew vañ
some jam	**de la confiture**
	duh la koñ-fee-tewr
some chips	**des frites**
	day freet
Do you have...?	**Est-ce que vous avez...?/**
	Vous avez...?
	es kuh voo za-vay...?/voo za-vay...?
Do you have	**Est-ce que vous avez une**
a room?	**chambre?**
	es kuh voo za-vay ewn shahñbr?

Do you have some milk?	**Vous avez du lait?**	voo za-vay dew leh?
I'd like...	**Je voudrais...**	zhuh voo-dreh...
We'd like...	**Nous voudrions...**	noo voo-dree-oñ...
I'd like an ice cream	**Je voudrais une glace**	zhuh voo-dreh ewn glas
We'd like to visit Paris	**Nous voudrions visiter Paris**	noo voo-dree-oñ vee-zee-tay pa-ree
Some more...	**Encore du/de la/des...**	ahñ-kor dew/duh la/day...
Another...	**Un/Une autre...**	uñ/ewn ohtr...
Some more bread	**Encore du pain**	ahñ-kor dew pañ
Some more soup	**Encore de la soupe**	ahñ-kor duh la soop
Some more glasses	**D'autres verres**	dohtr vehr
Another coffee	**Un autre café**	uñ ohtr ka-fay
Another beer	**Une autre bière**	ewn ohtr byehr
How much is it?	**C'est combien?**	say koñ-byañ?
How much is the room?	**C'est combien la chambre?**	say koñ-byañ la shahñbr?

large/small	**grand/petit** grahñ/puh-tee
with/without	**avec/sans** a-vek/sahñ
Where is/are...?	**Où est/sont...?** oo ay/soñ...?
the nearest	**le/la plus proche** luh/la plew prosh
How do I get...?	**Pour aller...?** poor a-lay...?
to the museum	**au musée** oh mew-zay
to the station	**à la gare** a la gar
to Brioude	**à Brioude** a bree-ood
There is/are...	**Il y a...** eel ya...
There isn't/ aren't any...	**Il n'y a pas de...** eel nya pa duh...
When...?	**Quand...?** kahñ...?
At what time...?	**À quelle heure...?** a kel ur...?
today	**aujourd'hui** oh-zhoor-dwee
tomorrow	**demain** duh-mañ

yesterday	**hier** ee-yehr
Can I...?	**Est-ce que je peux...?** es kuh zhuh puh...?
smoke	**fumer** few-may
What does this mean?	**Qu'est-ce que ça veut dire?** kes kuh sa vuh deer?

Signs and notices

entrée	entrance
sortie	exit
ouvert	open
fermé	closed
chaud	hot
froid	cold
tirez	pull
poussez	push
à droite	right
à gauche	left
eau potable	drinking water
à emporter	take-away

dégustation de vin	wine tasting
prière de...	please...
libre	free, vacant
occupé	engaged
caisse	cash desk
libre-service	self-service
toilettes	toilets
dames	ladies
hommes, messieurs	gents
hors service	out of order
à louer	for hire/to rent
à vendre	for sale
soldes	sale
baignade interdite	no swimming
sous-sol	basement
rez-de-chaussée	ground floor
ascenseur	lift
accès aux trains	to the trains
chambres	rooms available
complet	no vacancies
sortie de secours	emergency exit
sonnez	ring

appuyez	press
privé	private
arrêt	stop
billets	tickets
accueil	information
composter votre billet	validate your ticket
buffet	snacks
consigne	left luggage
défense de fumer	no smoking

Polite expressions

• •

There are two forms of address in French, formal (**vous**) and informal (**tu**). You should always stick to the formal until you are invited to **tutoyer** (use the informal **tu**).

The meal was delicious	**Le repas était délicieux** luh ruh-pa ay-teh day-lee-syuh
Thank you very much	**Je vous remercie** zhuh voo ruh-mehr-see
Delighted to meet you	**Enchanté(e)** ahñ-shahñ-tay
This is...	**Voici...** vwa-see...

| my husband/
my wife | **mon mari/ma femme**
moñ ma-ree/ma fam |
| Enjoy your
holiday! | **Passez de bonnes vacances!**
pa-say duh bon va-kahñs! |

Celebrations

• •

Christmas celebrations revolve around food as much as they do presents. They start on Christmas Eve (**réveillon de Noël**) with a lavish meal lasting many hours. The main course is usually goose, turkey, capon or white pudding followed by the traditional dessert, a **bûche de Noël** (Christmas log). Families start the celebrations with an **apéritif** before the meal accompanied by foie gras and elaborate **amuse-bouche** (nibbles). Champagne sometimes replaces the usual **apéritif** drinks.

I'd like to wish you a...	**Je vous souhaite un/une...** zhuh voo soo-eht uñ/ewn...
Merry Christmas!	**Joyeux Noël!** zhwa-yuh noh-el!
Happy New Year!	**Bonne année!** bon a-nay!
Happy Easter!	**Joyeuses Pâques!** zhwa-yuz pak!
Happy birthday!	**Bon anniversaire!** bon a-nee-vehr-sehr!

Have a good trip! **Bon voyage!**
boñ vwa-yazh!

Enjoy your meal! **Bon appétit!**
bon a-pay-tee!

Making friends

· ·

In this section we have used the informal **tu** for the questions.

FACE TO FACE

Comment tu t'appelles?
ko-mahñ tew ta-pel?
What's your name?

Je m'appelle...
zhuh ma-pel...
My name is...

Tu es d'où?
tew ay doo?
Where are you from?

Je suis anglais(e), de Londres
zhuh swee zahñ-gleh(z), duh loñdr
I am English, from London

Enchanté(e)!
ahñ-shahñ-tay!
Pleased to meet you!

De rien!
duh ryañ!
You're welcome!

How old are you?	**Quel âge as-tu?**	
	kel azh a tew?	
I'm ... years old	**J'ai ... ans**	
	zhay ... ahñ	
Are you French?	**Tu es français(e)?**	
	tew ay frahñ-seh(z)?	
I'm English/ Scottish/ American	**Je suis anglais(e)/ écossais(e)/américain(e)**	
	zhuh swee zahñ-gleh(z)/ zay-ko-seh(z)/za-mayree-kañ/ken	
England/English	**l'Angleterre** f**/anglais(e)**	
	ahñ-gluh-tehr/ahñ-gleh(z)	
Scotland/ Scottish	**l'Écosse** f**/écossais(e)**	
	ay-kos/ay-ko-seh(z)	
Wales/Welsh	**le Pays de Galles/gallois(e)**	
	pay-yee duh gal/ga-lwa(z)	
Ireland/Irish	**l'Irlande** f**/irlandais(e)**	
	eer-lahñd/eer-lahñ-deh(z)	
USA/American	**les États-Unis/américain(e)**	
	ay-ta-zew-nee/a-may-ree-kañ/ken	
Australia/ Australian	**l'Australie** f**/australien(ne)**	
	oh-stra-lee/oh-stra-lyañ/lee-en	
Where do you live?	**Où est-ce que tu habites?**	
	oo es kuh tew a-beet?	

Where do you live? (plural)	**Où est-ce que vous habitez?** oo es kuh voo za-bee-tay?
I live in London	**J'habite à Londres** zha-beet a loñdr
We live in Glasgow	**Nous habitons à Glasgow** noo za-bee-toñ a glaz-goh
I'm...	**Je suis...** zhuh swee...
single	**célibataire** say-lee-ba-tehr
married	**marié(e)** mar-yay
divorced	**divorcé(e)** dee-vor-say
I have...	**J'ai...** zhay...
a boyfriend	**un petit ami** uñ puh-tee-ta-mee
a girlfriend	**une petite amie** ewn puh-teet a-mee
I have a partner (male/female)	**J'ai un compagnon/ une compagne** zhay uñ koñ-pa-nyoñ/ ewn koñ-panyuh
I have ... children	**J'ai ... enfants** zhay ... ahñ-fahñ
I have no children	**Je n'ai pas d'enfants** zhuh nay pas dahñ-fahñ

I'm here on holiday/ on business/ for the weekend	**Je suis ici en vacances/ en voyage d'affaires/ en week-end** zhuh swee zee-see ahñ va-kahñs/ ahñ vwa-yazh da-fehr/ ahñ wee-kend

Work

. . . .

What work do you do?	**Qu'est-ce que vous faites comme travail?** kes kuh voo fet kom tra-va-yuh?
I'm...	**Je suis...** zhuh swee...
a doctor	**médecin** may-dsañ
a manager	**directeur** dee-rek-tur
a secretary	**secrétaire** suh-kray-tehr
I'm self-employed	**Je travaille à mon compte** zhuh tra-va-yuh a moñ koñt

Weather

....

temps variable tahñ va-ree-abl	changeable weather
beau boh	fine
temps orageux tahñ o-ra-zhuh	thundery weather

It's sunny	**Il y a du soleil** eel ya dew so-lay
It's raining	**Il pleut** eel pluh
It's snowing	**Il neige** eel nezh
It's windy	**Il y a du vent** eel ya dew vahñ
What a lovely day!	**Quelle belle journée!** kel bel zhoor-nay!
What awful weather!	**Quel mauvais temps!** kel moh-veh tahñ!
What will the weather be like tomorrow?	**Quel temps fera-t-il demain?** kel tahñ fuh-ra-teel duh-mañ?
Do you think it's going to rain?	**Vous croyez qu'il va pleuvoir?** voo krwa-yay keel va pluh-vwar?
It's very hot/cold	**Il fait très chaud/froid** eel feh treh shoh/frwa

25

Getting around

Asking the way

. . . .

en face de ahñ fas duh	opposite
à côté de a ko-tay duh	next to
près de preh duh	near to
le carrefour luh kar-foor	crossroads
le rond-point luh roñ-pwañ	roundabout

FACE TO FACE

Pardon, pour aller à la gare?
par-doñ, poor a-lay a la gar?
Excuse me, how do I get to the station?

Continuez tout droit, et après l'église, tournez à gauche/à droite
koñ-tee-new-ay too drwa, ay a-preh lay-gleez, toor-nay a gohsh/a drwat
Keep straight on, and after the church turn left/right

C'est loin?
say lwañ?
Is it far?

Non, c'est à deux cents mètres/à cinq minutes
noñ, say ta duh sahñ metr/a sañk mee-newt
No, it's 200 yards/five minutes away

Merci!
mehr-see!
Thank you!

De rien!
duh ryañ!
You're welcome!

We're looking for...	**Nous cherchons...** noo shehr-shoñ...
Can we walk there?	**On peut y aller à pied?** oñ puh ee a-lay a pyay?
We're lost	**Nous nous sommes perdu(e)s** noo noo som pehr-dew
Is this the right way to...?	**C'est la bonne direction pour...?** say la bon dee-rek-syoñ poor...?
Can you show me on the map?	**Pouvez-vous me montrer sur la carte/le plan?** poo-vay voo me moñ-tray sewr la kart/luh plahñ?

27

YOU MAY HEAR...

C'est indiqué say tañ-dee-kay	It's signposted
C'est au coin de la rue say toh kwañ duh la rew	It's on the corner of the street
C'est là-bas say la-ba	It's over there

Bus and coach

• •

Public transport is free for children under four.
Children between four and eleven pay half price.

FACE TO FACE

Excusez-moi, quel est le bus pour le centre-ville?
eks-kew-zay-mwa, kel ay luh bews poor luh sahñtr veel?
Excuse me, which bus goes to the centre?

Le 15
luh kañz
Number 15

Où est l'arrêt?
oo ay la-reh?
Where is the bus stop?

Là-bas, à gauche
la-ba, a gohsh
There, on the left

Où est-ce que je peux acheter des tickets de bus?
oo es kuh zhuh puh ash-tay day tee-keh duh bews?
Where can I buy bus tickets?

Là-bas, au distributeur
la-ba, oh dees-tree-bew-tur
Over there, at the ticket machine

Is there a bus to...?	**Est-ce qu'il y a un bus pour...?** es keel ya uñ bews poor...?
Where do I catch the bus to go to...?	**Où est-ce qu'on prend le bus pour aller à/au (etc.)...?** oo es koñ prahñ luh bews poor a-lay a/oh...?
How much is it...?	**C'est combien pour aller...?** say koñ-byañ poor a-lay...?
to the centre	**dans le centre** dahñ luh sahñtr
to the beach	**à la plage** a la plazh
to the shops	**aux magasins** oh ma-ga-zañ
to Montmartre	**à Montmartre** a moñ-martr

| A child's ticket | **Un billet tarif enfant** |
| | un bee-yeh ta-reef ahñ-fahñ |

| How frequent are the buses to...? | **Les bus pour ... passent tous les combien?** |
| | lay bews poor ... pas too lay koñ-byañ? |

| When is the first/ the last bus to...? | **À quelle heure part le premier/le dernier bus pour...?** |
| | a kel ur par luh pruh-myay/ luh dehr-nyay bews poor...? |

| Could you tell me when to get off? | **Pourriez-vous me dire quand descendre?** |
| | poo-ree-ay-voo muh deer kahñ deh-sahñdr? |

| This is my stop | **C'est mon arrêt** |
| | say mon a-reh |

| coach | **le car** |
| | kar |

| shuttle bus | **la navette** |
| | na-vet |

YOU MAY HEAR...

| **Prenez le métro, c'est plus rapide** pruh-nay luh may-troh, say plew ra-peed | Take the metro, it's quicker |

Metro

. . . .

There are metro services in Paris, Lyon, Marseille, Lille, Toulouse and Rennes. In Paris, ticket options include **un carnet de dix tickets** (a book of ten tickets), which can be used on the metro, bus and **RER** (a network of high-speed trains connecting Paris and the suburbs). You can also buy a **PARIS VISITE**, a ticket lasting 1–5 days that allows unlimited travel on all forms of public transport as well as discounts for certain tourist attractions.

entrée ahñ-tray	entrance
sortie sor-tee	way out/exit
la ligne de métro la lee-nyuh duh may-troh	metro line
en direction de... ahñ dee-rek-syoñ duh...	in the direction of...
correspondance ko-reh-spoñ-dahñs	connecting line

Where is the nearest metro?	**Où est la station de métro la plus proche?** oo ay la sta-syoñ duh may-troh la plew prosh?
I'm going to...	**Je vais à...** zhuh veh a...

31

How does the ticket machine work?	**Comment marche le guichet automatique?** ko-mahñ marsh luh gee-sheh oh-toh-ma-teek?
Do you have a map of the metro?	**Vous avez un plan du métro?** voo za-vay uñ plahñ dew may-troh?
How do I get to...?	**Pour aller à/au (etc.)...?** poor a-lay a/oh...?
Do I have to change?	**Est-ce qu'il faut changer?** es keel foh shahñ-zhay?
Which line is it for...?	**C'est quelle ligne pour...?** say kel lee-nyuh poor...?
In which direction?	**Dans quelle direction?** dahñ kel dee-rek-syoñ?
What is the next stop?	**Quel est le prochain arrêt?** kel ay luh pro-shañ na-reh?

Train

Before you catch your train, you must validate your ticket in one of the machines situated on the platforms, which carry the warning **n'oubliez pas de composter votre billet**. Failing to do so could result in a fine. The **TGV** (train à grande vitesse) is a high-speed train network that runs between major French towns/cities and into neighbouring countries. It is expensive, but reduced-price tickets called

TGV PREM'S are available if booked several weeks in advance. Other services that use TGV trains include the Eurostar (connecting Paris with London), the Thalys (connecting Paris with Lille, Brussels and Amsterdam) and the TGV Lyria (connecting Paris with the main Swiss cities).

horaire o-rehr	timetable
circuler seer-kew-lay	to operate
dimanches et fêtes dee-mahñsh ay fet	Sundays and holidays
accès aux quais/aux voies ak-seh oh keh/oh vwa	to the platforms
le billet électronique bee-yeh ay-lek-tro-neek	e-ticket
la réservation sur Internet ray-zehr-va-syoñ sewr añ-tehr-net	e-booking

FACE TO FACE

Quand part le prochain train pour...?
kahñ par luh pro-shañ trañ poor...?
When is the next train to...?

À 17 heures 10
a dee-set ur dees
At ten past five

Deux billets pour...
duh bee-yeh poor...
Two tickets to...

Aller simple ou aller-retour?
a-lay sañpl oo a-lay-ruh-toor?
Single or return?

First class/ Second class	**Première classe/ Deuxième classe** pruh myehr klas/duh-zyem klas
I booked online	**J'ai réservé sur Internet** zhay ray-zehr-vay sewr añ-tehr-net
Is there a supplement to pay?	**Y a-t-il un supplément à payer?** ee a-teel uñ sew-play-mahñ a pay-yay?
I want to book a seat on the TGV to Nîmes	**Je voudrais réserver une place dans le TGV pour Nîmes** zhuh voo-dreh ray-zehr-vay ewn plas dahñ luh tay-zhay-vay poor neem
When is the train to...?	**Le train pour ... est à quelle heure?** luh trañ poor ... ay ta kel ur?
the first/the last	**le premier/le dernier** luh pruh myay/luh dehr-nyay
When does it arrive in...?	**À quelle heure arrive-t-il à...?** a kel ur a-reev-teel a...?

Do I have to change?	**Est-ce qu'il faut changer?** es keel foh shahñ-zhay?
Which platform does it leave from?	**Il part de quel quai?** eel par duh kel kay?
Is this the right platform for the train to Paris?	**C'est le bon quai pour le train de Paris?** say luh boñ kay poor luh trañ duh pa-ree?
Is this the train for...?	**C'est le train pour...?** say luh trañ poor...?
When does it leave?	**Il part à quelle heure?** eel par a kel ur?
Does the train stop at...?	**Est-ce que le train s'arrête à...?** es kuh luh trañ sa-ret a...?
Where do I change for...?	**Où dois-je changer pour...?** oo dwa-zhuh shahñ-zhay poor...?
Please tell me when we get to...	**S'il vous plaît, prévenez-moi quand nous serons à...** seel voo pleh, pray-vnay mwa kañ noo suh-roñ za...
Is this seat free?	**Cette place est-elle libre?** set plas ay-tel leebr?
Excuse me	**Excusez-moi** eks-kew-zay-mwa
Sorry!	**Pardon!** par-doñ!

Taxi

The main taxi companies in Paris are **Les Taxis bleus**, **Alphataxi** and **G7**. A French taxi is available for hire when the **taxi** sign is lit up in white or green. If a taxi is occupied, the sign is switched off or lit up in red.

la station de taxis la sta-syoñ duh tak-see	taxi rank

I want a taxi	**Je voudrais un taxi** zhuh voo-dreh uñ tak-see
Where can I get a taxi?	**Où est-ce que je peux prendre un taxi?** oo es kuh zhuh puh prahñdr uñ tak-see?
Could you order me a taxi?	**Pouvez-vous m'appeler un taxi?** poo-vay voo ma-play uñ tak-see?
How much is it going to cost to go to...?	**Combien ça va coûter pour aller à/au (etc.)...?** koñ-byañ sa va koo-tay poor a-lay a/oh...?
to the town centre	**au centre-ville** oh sahñtr-veel
to the station	**à la gare** a la gar

to the airport	**à l'aéroport**
	a la-ay-ro-por
to this address	**à cette adresse**
	a set a-dres
Keep the change	**Gardez la monnaie**
	gar-day la mo-neh
Sorry, I don't have any change	**Je suis désolé(e), je n'ai pas de monnaie**
	zhuh swee day-zo-lay, zhuh nay pa duh mo-neh
Is it far?	**C'est loin?**
	say lwañ?

Boat and ferry

When is the next boat/ferry to...?	**À quelle heure part le prochain bateau/ferry pour...?**
	a kel ur par luh pro-shañ ba-toh/feh-ree poor...?
Have you a timetable?	**Vous avez un horaire?**
	voo za-vay uñ noh-rehr?
Is there a car ferry to...?	**Est-ce qu'il y a un car ferry pour...?**
	es keel ya uñ car feh-ree poor...?
How much is...?	**C'est combien...?**
	seh koñ-byañ...?
a single	**un aller simple**
	uñ na-lay sañpl

37

a return	**un aller-retour** uñ na-lay-ruh-toor
How much is it for a car and ... people?	**C'est combien pour une voiture et ... personnes?** say koñ-byañ poor ewn vwa-tewr ay ... pehr-son?
How long does the crossing take?	**La traversée dure combien de temps?** la tra-vehr-say dewr koñ-byañ duh tahñ?
Where does the boat leave from?	**D'où part le bateau?** doo par luh ba-toh?
When is the first/last boat?	**Quand part le premier/dernier bateau?** kahñ par luh pruh-myay/dehr-nyay ba-toh?
What time do we get to...?	**On arrive à quelle heure à...?** on a-reev a kel ur a...?
Is there somewhere to eat on the boat?	**Est-ce qu'on peut manger sur le bateau?** es koñ puh mahñ-zhay sewr luh ba-toh?

Air travel

. . . .

The three main airports in Paris are **Paris Charles-de-Gaulle** (also called **Roissy**), **Paris Orly** and **Beauvais-Tillé**. The latter is the airport used by most budget airlines for flights to Paris. Despite being referred to as **Paris-Beauvais**, this airport is actually more than 50 miles outside the city.

How do I get to the airport?	**Comment fait-on pour aller à l'aéroport?** ko-mahñ fay toñ poor a-lay a la-ay-ro-por?
How long does it take to get to the airport?	**On met combien de temps pour aller à l'aéroport?** oñ meh koñ-byañ duh tahñ poor a-lay a la-ay-ro-por?
checked luggage	**les bagages enregistrés** ba-gazh ahñ-ruh-zhee-stray
hand luggage	**les bagages à main** ba-gazh a mañ
Is there an airport bus to the city centre?	**Est-ce qu'il y a une navette pour aller au centre-ville?** es keel ya ewn na-vet poor a-lay oh sahñtr-veel?
Where do I check in for...?	**Où est l'enregistrement pour...?** oo ay lahñ-ruh-zhee-struh-mahñ poor...?

Where is the luggage for the flight from...?	**Où sont les bagages du vol en provenance de...?** oo soñ lay ba-gazh dew vol ahñ pro-vnahñs duh...?
Which is the departure gate for the flight to...?	**Quelle est la porte d'embarquement pour le vol à destination de...?** kel ay la port dahñ-bar-kuh-mahñ poor luh vol a des-tee-na-syoñ duh...?
Where can I print my ticket?	**Où est-ce que je peux imprimer mon billet?** oo es kuh zhuh puh añ-pree-may moñ bee-yeh?
I have my boarding pass on my smartphone	**J'ai ma carte d'embarquement sur mon smartphone** zhay ma kart dahñ-bar-kuh-mahñ sewr moñ smart-fon

YOU MAY HEAR...

L'embarquement aura lieu porte numéro... lahñ-bar-kuh-mahñ oh-ra lyuh port new-may-ro...	Boarding will take place at gate number...
Présentez-vous immédiatement porte numéro... pray-zahñ-tay voo ee-may-dyat-mahñ port new-may-ro...	Go immediately to gate number...
Votre vol a du retard votr vol a dew ruh-tar	Your flight is delayed

Liquides interdits lee-keed añ-tehr-dee	No liquids
Vos bagages dépassent le poids maximal autorisé voh ba-gazh day-pass luh pwa mak-see-mal oh-toh-ree-zay	Your luggage exceeds the maximum weight

Customs control

• •

With the Single European Market, European Union (EU) citizens are subject only to spot checks and can go through the blue customs channel (unless they have goods to declare). There is no restriction, in either quantity or value, on goods purchased by EU travellers in another EU country provided that they are for personal use.

contrôle des passeports koñ-trol day pas-por	passport control
UE (Union européenne) ew uh	EU (European Union)
autres passeports ohtr pas-por	other passports
douane dwan	customs

Getting around

41

Do I have to pay duty on this?	**Est-ce que je dois payer des droits de douane sur ça?** es kuh zhuh dwa pay-yay day drwa duh dwan sewr sa?
It is for my own personal use	**C'est pour mon usage personnel** say poor mon ew-zazh pehr-so-nel
We are on our way to... (if in transit through a country)	**Nous allons en/au/aux...** noo za-loñ ahñ/oh/oh...

Car hire

• •

To hire a car in France, you must be at least 21 years old and have held a driving licence for a year or more.

le permis de conduire luh pehr-mee duh koñ-dweer	driving licence
l'assurance la-sew-rahñs	insurance
la franchise la frahñ-sheez	excess

| I want to hire a car | **Je voudrais louer une voiture** zhuh voo-dreh loo-ay ewn vwa-tewr |

for ... days	**pour ... jours**
	poor ... zhoor
for the weekend	**pour le week-end**
	poor luh wee-kend
What are your rates...?	**Quels sont vos tarifs...?**
	kel soñ voh ta-reef...?
per day	**par jour**
	par zhoor
per week	**par semaine**
	par suh-men
Is there a mileage (kilometre) charge?	**Est-ce que le kilométrage est en plus?**
	es kuh luh kee-lo-may-trazh ay tahñ plews?
Does the price include comprehensive insurance?	**Est-ce que le prix comprend l'assurance tous-risques?**
	es kuh luh pree koñ-prahñ la-sew-rahñs too reesk?
Do I have to return the car here?	**Est-ce que je dois rendre la voiture ici?**
	es kuh zhuh dwa rahñdr la vwa-tewr ee-see?
By what time?	**Vers quelle heure?**
	vehr kel ur?
I'd like to leave it in...	**Je voudrais la laisser à...**
	zhuh voo-dreh la leh-say a...
What do I do if we break down?	**Que dois-je faire en cas de panne?**
	kuh dwa-zhuh fehr ahñ ka duh pan?

Veuillez rendre la voiture avec un plein d'essence vuh-yay rahñdr la vwa-tewr a-vek uñ plañ deh-sahñs	Please return the car with a full tank

Driving

• • • • • • • • • • • • • • • • • • • •

I am looking for a car park	**Je cherche un parking** zhuh shehrsh uñ par-keeng
Do I need to pay?	**Il faut payer?** eel foh pay-ay?
Can I park here?	**On peut se garer ici?** oñ puh suh ga-ray ee-see?
Can you show me on the map?	**Pouvez-vous me montrer sur la carte/le plan?** poo-vay voo muh moñ-tray sewr la kart/luh plahñ?

When driving in Paris, try not to let yourself get stressed by the discourteous driving you may encounter! If you visit in August, you will find that many Parisians have left the city and it will be easier to get around.

Petrol

• • • • • • • • • • • • • • • • • • •

sans plomb sahñ ploñ	unleaded
diesel/gasoil dee-eh-zel/ga-zwal	diesel

Fill it up, please	**Le plein, s'il vous plaît** luh plañ, seel voo pleh
Please check the oil/the water	**Pouvez-vous vérifier l'huile/l'eau?** poo-vay voo vay-ree-fyay lweel/loh?
...euros' worth of unleaded petrol	**...euros d'essence sans plomb** ...uh-roh deh-sahñs sahñ ploñ
Pump number...	**La pompe numéro...** la pomp new-may-roh...
Can you check the tyre pressure?	**Pouvez-vous vérifier la pression des pneus?** Poo-vay voo vay-ree-fyay la preh-syoñ day pnuh?
Where do I pay?	**Où dois-je payer?** oo dwa-zhuh pay-yay?
Do you take credit cards?	**Vous acceptez les cartes de crédit?** voo zak-sep-tay lay kart duh kray-dee?

Breakdown

●●●●●●●●●●●●●●●●●●●●

assistance automobile a-sees-tahñs oh-toh-mo-beel	breakdown assistance

Can you help me?
Pouvez-vous m'aider?
poo-vay voo may-day?

My car has broken down
Ma voiture est en panne
ma vwa-tewr ay tahñ pan

I can't start the car
Je n'arrive pas à démarrer
zhuh na-reev pa a day-ma-ray

I've run out of petrol
Je suis en panne d'essence
zhuh swee ahñ pan deh-sahñs

Is there a garage near here?
Il y a un garage près d'ici?
eel ya uñ ga-razh preh dee-see?

Can you tow me to the nearest garage?
Pouvez-vous me remorquer jusqu'au garage le plus proche?
Poo-vay voo muh ruh-mor-kay zhew-skoh ga-razh luh plew prosh?

Do you have parts for a...?
(make of car)
Avez-vous des pièces de rechange pour une...?
a-vay voo day pyes duh ruh-shahñzh poor ewn...?

There's something wrong with the...
J'ai un problème avec le/la/les...
zhay uñ prob-lem a-vek luh/la/lay...

46

Car parts

● ●

The ... doesn't work	**Le/La/L' ... ne marche pas**	luh/la/l ... nuh marsh pa
The ... don't work	**Les ... ne marchent pas**	lay ... nuh marsh pa

accelerator	**l'accélérateur**	ak-say-lay-ra-tur
battery	**la batterie**	ba-tree
bonnet	**le capot**	ka-poh
brakes	**les freins**	frañ
choke	**le starter**	star-tehr
clutch	**l'embrayage**	ahñ-bray-yazh
distributor	**le delco**	del-koh
engine	**le moteur**	mo-tur
exhaust pipe	**le pot d'échappement**	poh day-shap-mahñ
fuse	**le fusible**	few-zeebl
gears	**les vitesses**	vee-tes
handbrake	**le frein à main**	frañ a mañ
headlights	**les phares**	far
ignition	**l'allumage**	a-lew-mazh
indicator	**le clignotant**	klee-nyo-tahñ
points	**les vis platinées**	vees pla-tee-nay
radiator	**le radiateur**	ra-dya-tur

47

reversing lights	**les phares de recul**	far duh ruh-kewl
seat belt	**la ceinture de sécurité**	sañ-tewr duh say-kewr-eetay
sidelights	**les veilleuses**	vay-yuhz
spare wheel	**la roue de secours**	roo duh skoor
spark plugs	**les bougies**	boo-zhee
steering	**la direction**	dee-rek-syoñ
steering wheel	**le volant**	vo-lahñ
tyre	**le pneu**	pnuh
wheel	**la roue**	roo
windscreen	**le pare-brise**	par-breez
windscreen washers	**le lave-glace**	lav-glas
windscreen wiper	**l'essuie-glace**	es-wee-glas

Road signs

customs

toll station for motorway

give way

slow down

one way

diversion

priority road

north

west   east

south

Getting around

libre
spaces

complet
full

STATIONNEMENT
INTERDIT

no parking

ALLUMEZ
VOS
FEUX

switch on
your lights

FRANCE

50

90

130

speeds are in
kilometres per hour

AUTOROUTE
motorway

Staying somewhere

Hotel (booking)

• •

You can book accommodation over the internet using the French Tourist Office website, **www.franceguide.fr**.

a single room	**une chambre pour une personne** ewn shahñbr poor ewn pehr-son
a double room	**une chambre pour deux personnes** ewn shahñbr poor duh pehr-son
with bath	**avec bain** a-vek bañ
with shower	**avec douche** a-vek doosh
with a double bed	**avec un grand lit** a-vek uñ grahñ lit
twin beds	**à deux lits** a duh lee
a cot	**un lit d'enfant** uñ lee dahñ-fahñ

51

Do you have any bedrooms on the ground floor?	**Avez-vous des chambres au rez-de-chaussée?** a-vay voo day shahñbr oh ray duh shoh-say?
Do you have a room for tonight?	**Est-ce que vous avez une chambre pour cette nuit?** es kuh voo za-vay ewn shahñbr poor set nwee?
How much is it per night/ per week?	**C'est combien la nuit/ la semaine?** say koñ-byañ la nwee/la suh-men?
I'll arrive at...	**J'arriverai à...** zha-ree-vuh-ray a...
Could you recommend a good hotel?	**Pouvez-vous me conseiller un bon hôtel?** poo-vay voo muh koñ-say-yay uñ boñ noh-tel?
not too expensive	**pas trop cher** pa troh shehr

FACE TO FACE

Je voudrais (réserver) une chambre pour une/deux personnes
zhuh voo-dreh (ray-zehr-vay) ewn shahñbr poor ewn/duh pehr-son
I'd like (to book) a single/double room

C'est pour combien de nuits?
say poor koñ-byañ duh nwee?
For how many nights?

Pour une nuit/... nuits
poor ewn nwee/... nwee
For one night/... nights

Du... au...
dew... oh...
From... till...

C'est pour combien de personnes?
say poor koñ-byañ duh pehr-son?
For how many people?

Pour une personne/... personnes
poor ewn pehr-son/... pehr-son
For one person/... people

YOU MAY HEAR...	
C'est complet say koñ-pleh	We're full
Votre nom, s'il vous plaît? votr noñ, seel voo pleh?	Your name, please?
Veuillez confirmer... vuh-yay koñ-feer-may...	Please confirm...
par e-mail par ee-mehl	by e-mail
par téléphone par tay-lay-fon	by phone
Vous arriverez à quelle heure? voo za-ree-vuh-ray a kel ur?	What time will you arrive?

Hotel desk

• •

You generally have to fill in a registration form (**fiche d'hôtel**) and give your passport number on arrival.

I booked a room	**J'ai réservé une chambre** zhay ray-zehr-vay ewn shahñbr
My name is...	**Je m'appelle...** zhuh ma-pel...
I reserved the room(s) online	**J'ai réservé cette chambre (ces chambres) en ligne** zhay ray-zehr-vay set shahñbr (say shahñbr) oñ lee-nyuh
Does the price include breakfast?	**Est-ce que le petit-déjeuner est inclus dans le prix?** es kuh luh puh-tee day-zhuh-nay ay-tañ-kloo dahñ luh pree?
Is there a hotel restaurant/bar?	**Est-ce qu'il y a un restaurant/ un bar à l'hôtel?** es keel ya uñ reh-stoh-rahñ/ uñ bar a loh-tel?
Where can I park the car?	**Où est-ce que je peux garer la voiture?** oo es kuh zhuh puh ga-ray la vwa-tewr?
What time is...?	**À quelle heure est...?** a kel ur eh...?

54

dinner	**le dîner** luh dee-nay
breakfast	**le petit-déjeuner** luh puh-tee day-zhuh-nay
The key, please	**La clé/clef, s'il vous plaît** la klay, seel voo pleh
Room number...	**Chambre numéro...** shahñbr new-may-ro...
I'm leaving tomorrow	**Je pars demain** zhuh par duh-mañ
Where is the lift?	**Où est l'ascenseur?** oo eh la-sahñ-sur?

Camping

ordures or-dewr	rubbish
eau potable oh po-tabl	drinking water
bloc sanitaire blok sa-nee-tehr	washing facilities

| Is there a restaurant on the campsite? | **Y a-t-il un restaurant dans le camping?**
ee a-teel uñ re-sto-rahñ dahñ luh kahñ-peeng? |

Do you have any vacancies?	**Vous avez des emplacements de libres?** Voo za-vay day zahñ-plas-mahñ duh leebr?
Are there any toilets for disabled people?	**Est-ce qu'il y a des toilettes pour handicapés?** es keel ya day twa-let poorahñ-dee-ka-pay
Does the price include...?	**Est-ce que le prix comprend...?** es kuh luh pree koñ-prahñ...?
hot water	**l'eau chaude** loh shohd
electricity	**l'électricité** lay-lek-tree-see-tay
We'd like to stay for ... nights	**Nous voudrions rester ... nuits** noo voo-dree-yoñ res-tay ... nwee
How much is it per night...?	**C'est combien la nuit...?** say koñ-byañ la nwee...?
for a tent	**pour une tente** poor ewn tahñt
for a caravan	**pour une caravane** poor ewn ka-ra-van

Self-catering

• •

You can find a variety of self-catering accommodation on **www.gites-de-france.com**, the website of the national Gîtes de France federation. Another popular website for private accommodation is **www.airbnb.fr**.

Who do we contact if there are problems?	**Qui devons-nous contacter en cas de problème?** kee duh-voñ noo koñ-tak-tay ahñ ka duh prob-lehm?
How does the heating work?	**Comment marche le chauffage?** ko-mahñ marsh luh shoh-fazh?
Is there always hot water?	**Est-ce qu'il y a de l'eau chaude en permanence?** es keel ya duh loh shohd ahñ per-ma-nahñs?
Where is the nearest supermarket?	**Où est le supermarché le plus proche?** oo ay luh sew-pehr-mar-shay luh plew prosh?
Where do we leave the rubbish?	**Où est-ce qu'il faut mettre les ordures?** oo es keel foh metr lay zor-dewr?
recycling	**le recyclage** ruh-see-klazh

Shopping

Shopping phrases

· ·

French shop opening hours are approximately
9 a.m. to 7 p.m., but many shops (except those in
Paris) close between 12 and 2 p.m. Most are closed
on Sundays and some also on Mondays.

FACE TO FACE

Qu'est-ce que vous désirez?
kes kuh voo day-zee-ray?
What would you like?

Est-ce que vous avez...?
es kuh voo za-vay...?
Do you have...?

Oui, bien sûr. Voilà. Et avec ceci?
wee, byañ sewr. vwa-la. ay a-vek suh-see?
Yes, certainly. Here you are. Anything else?

Where is...?	**Où est...?** oo ay...?
Where can I buy...?	**Où est-ce qu'on peut acheter...?** oo es koñ puh ash-tay...?

toys	**des jouets** day zhoo-ay	
gifts	**des cadeaux** day ka-doh	
Where is the ... department?	**Où se trouve le rayon...?** oo suh troov luh ray-yoñ...?	
perfume	**parfumerie** par-few-mree	
jewellery	**bijouterie** bee-zhoo-tree	

Shops

. . . .

magasin ma-ga-zañ	shop
soldes sold	sale
un acheté, un gratuit uñ nash-tay, uñ gra-twee	buy one, get one free

baker's	**la boulangerie**	boo-lahñzh-ree
bookshop	**la librairie**	lee-breh-ree
butcher's	**la boucherie**	boo-shree
cake shop	**la pâtisserie**	pa-tee-sree
cheese shop	**la fromagerie**	fro-mazh-ree
clothes shop	**la boutique de vêtements**	boo-teek duh vetmahñ

dry-cleaner's	le pressing	pres-eeng
gift shop	la boutique de cadeaux	boo-teek duh ka-doh
grocer's	l'épicerie	ay-pees-ree
hairdresser's	chez le coiffeur/ la coiffeuse	shay luh kwa-fur/ la kwa-fuz
hypermarket	l'hypermarché	ee-pehr-mar-shay
jeweller's	la bijouterie	bee-zhoot-ree
market	le marché	mar-shay
pharmacy/ chemist's	la pharmacie	far-ma-see
self-service	le libre-service	leebr-sehr-vees
shoe shop	le magasin de chaussures	ma-ga-zañ duh shoh-sewr
souvenir shop	la boutique de souvenirs	boo-teek duh soov-neer
supermarket	le supermarché	sew-pehr-mar-shay
tobacconist's	le tabac	ta-ba

Food (general)

• •

baguette	la baguette	ba-get
bread	le pain	pañ
bread roll	le petit pain	puh-tee pañ
butter	le beurre	bur

cheese	**le fromage**	fro-mazh
chicken	**le poulet**	poo-leh
coffee (instant)	**le café (instantané)**	ka-fay (añ-stahñ-ta-nay)
cream	**la crème**	krem
crisps	**les chips**	sheeps
eggs	**les œufs**	uh
fish	**le poisson**	pwa-soñ
flour	**la farine**	fa-reen
ham (cooked)	**le jambon cuit**	zhahñ-boñ kwee
ham (cured)	**le jambon cru**	zhahñ-boñ kru
honey	**le miel**	myel
hot chocolate	**le chocolat en poudre**	sho-ko-la ahñ poodr
jam	**la confiture**	koñ-fee-tewr
margarine	**la margarine**	mar-ga-reen
marmalade	**la confiture d'orange**	koñ-fee-tewr do-rahñzh
milk	**le lait**	leh
oil	**l'huile**	weel
orange juice	**le jus d'orange**	zhew do-rahñzh
pasta	**les pâtes**	pat
pepper	**le poivre**	pwavr
rice	**le riz**	ree
salt	**le sel**	sel

sugar	**le sucre**	sewkr
tea	**le thé**	tay
yoghurt	**le yaourt**	ya-oort

Food (fruit and veg)

Fruit

fruit	**les fruits**	frwee
apples	**les pommes**	pom
bananas	**les bananes**	ba-nan
cherries	**les cerises**	suh-reez
grapefruit	**le pamplemousse**	pahñ-pluh-moos
grapes	**les raisins**	reh-zañ
lemon	**le citron**	see-troñ
melon	**le melon**	muh-loñ
nectarines	**les nectarines**	nek-ta-reen
oranges	**les oranges**	o-rahñzh
peaches	**les pêches**	pesh
pears	**les poires**	pwahr
pineapple	**l'ananas**	a-na-nas
plums	**les prunes**	prewn
raspberries	**les framboises**	frahñ-bwaz
strawberries	**les fraises**	frez

Vegetables

vegetables	**les légumes**	lay-gewm
carrots	**les carottes**	ka-rot
cauliflower	**le chou-fleur**	shoo-flur
courgettes	**les courgettes**	koor-zhet
French beans	**les haricots verts**	a-ree-koh vehr
garlic	**l'ail**	a-yuh
lettuce	**la laitue**	leh-tew
mushrooms	**les champignons**	shahñ-pee-nyoñ
onions	**les oignons**	o-nyoñ
peas	**les petits pois**	puh-tee pwa
peppers	**les poivrons**	pwa-vroñ
potatoes	**les pommes de terre**	pom duh tehr
spinach	**les épinards**	ay-pee-nar
tomatoes	**les tomates**	to-mat

Clothes

• •

Size for clothes is **la taille** (ta-yuh); for shoes it is
la pointure (pwañ-tewr).

FACE TO FACE

Est-ce que je peux l'essayer?
es kuh zhuh puh leh-say-yay?
May I try this on?

Certainement, par ici, s'il vous plaît
sehr-ten-mahñ, par ee-see, seel voo pleh
Certainly, please come this way

L'avez-vous en plus grand/en plus petit?
la-vay voo ahñ plew grahñ/ahñ plew puh-tee?
Do you have it in a bigger size/in a smaller size?

Désolé(e), je n'ai que cette taille dans ce colori
day-zo-lay, zhuh nay kuh set ta-yuh dahñ suh ko-lo-ree
Sorry, we only have this size in this colour

Do you have this in any other colours?	**Est-ce que vous l'avez dans d'autres coloris?** es kuh voo la-vay dahñ dohtr ko-lo-ree?
It's too...	**C'est trop...** say troh...
short	**court** koor

long	**long** loñ	
I'm just looking	**Je regarde seulement** zhuh ruh-gard suhl-mahñ	
I'll take it	**Je le/la prends** zhuh luh/la prahñ	

YOU MAY HEAR...

Quelle pointure faites-vous? kel pwañ-tewr feht voo?	What shoe size do you take?
Quelle est votre taille? kel eh votr ta-yuh?	What size (clothes) are you?

Clothes (articles)

• • • • • • • • • • • • • • • •

le coton luh ko-toñ	cotton
la soie la swa	silk
la dentelle la dahñ-tel	lace
la laine la lehn	wool

blouse	**le chemisier**	shuh-mee-zyay
bra	**le soutien-gorge**	soo-tyañ gorzh
coat	**le manteau**	mahñ-toh

dress	la robe	rob
gloves	les gants	gahñ
hat	le chapeau	sha-poh
jacket	la veste	vest
knickers	la culotte, le slip	kew-lot, sleep
nightdress	la chemise de nuit	shuh-meez duh nwee
pyjamas	le pyjama	pee-zha-ma
raincoat	l'imperméable	añ-pehr-may-abl
sandals	les sandales	sahñ-dal
scarf (silk)	le foulard	foo-lar
scarf (woollen)	l'écharpe	ay-sharp
shirt	la chemise	shuh-meez
shoes	les chaussures	shoh-sewr
shorts	le short	short
skirt	la jupe	zhewp
socks	les chaussettes	shoh-set
suit (woman's)	le tailleur	ta-yur
suit (man's)	le costume	kos-tewm
swimsuit	le maillot de bain	ma-yoh duh bañ
tights	les collants	ko-lahñ
t-shirt	le t-shirt	tee-shurt
tracksuit	le survêtement	sewr-vet-mahñ
trainers	les baskets	bas-ket
trousers	le pantalon	pahñ-ta-loñ

Maps and guides

Do you have...?	**Avez-vous...?** a-vay vooz...?
a map of the town	**un plan de la ville** uñ plahñ duh la veel
a map of the region	**une carte de la région** ewn kart duh la ray-zhyoñ
Can you show me where ... is on the map/town plan?	**Pouvez-vous me montrer où est ... sur la carte/le plan?** poo-vay voo muh moñ-tray oo eh ... sewr la kart/luh plahñ?
Do you have a guide book/ leaflet in English?	**Vous avez un guide/une brochure en anglais?** voo za-vay uñ geed/ewn bro-shewr ahñ nahñ-gleh?

Post office

Smaller post offices generally shut for lunch (12 to 2 p.m.).

la poste	la post	post office
timbres	tañbr	stamps

Is there a post office near here?	**Il y a un bureau de poste près d'ici?**
	eel ya uñ bewr-oh duh post preh dee-see?
When does it open?	**Il ouvre à quelle heure?**
	eel oovr a kel ur?
Which counter is it...?	**C'est quel guichet...?**
	say kel gee-shay...?
for stamps	**pour les timbres**
	poor lay tañbr
for parcels	**pour les colis**
	poor lay ko-lee
Three stamps for postcards to Great Britain	**Trois timbres pour cartes postales pour la Grande-Bretagne**
	trwa tañbr poor kart pos-tal poor la grahñd bruh-ta-nyuh
How much is it to send this parcel?	**C'est combien pour envoyer ce colis?**
	say koñ-byañ poor ahñ-vwa-yay suh ko-lee?

YOU MAY HEAR...

| **Vous pouvez acheter des timbres au tabac** | You can buy stamps at the tobacconist's |
| voo poo-vay ash-tay day tañbr oh ta-ba | |

68

Technology

• •

la carte mémoire kart may-mwar	memory card
imprimer añ-pree-may	to print
l'appareil (photo) numérique a-pa-ray (foh-toh) new-may-reek	digital camera
la cigarette électronique see-ga-ret ay-lek-tro-neek	e-cigarette

Do you have batteries for...?
Avez-vous des piles pour...?
a-vay voo day peel poor...?

this camera
cet appareil
set a-pa-ray

Do you have a memory card for...?
Avez-vous une carte mémoire pour...?
a-vay voo ewn kart may-mwar poor...?

this digital camera
cet appareil numérique
set a-pa-ray new-may-reek

Can you repair...?	**Pouvez-vous réparer...?**
	poo-vay voo ray-pa-ray...?
my screen	**mon écran** moñ ay-krahñ
my keypad	**mon clavier** moñ kla-vyay
my lens	**mon objectif** moñ ob-zhek-teef
my charger	**mon chargeur** moñ shar-zhur
I want to print my photos	**Je voudrais imprimer mes photos** zhuh voo-dreh añ-pree-may may foh-toh
I have it on my USB	**Je l'ai sur ma clé USB** zhuh lay sewr ma clay oo-es-bay
I have it on my e-mail	**Je l'ai sur mon e-mail** zhuh lay sewr moñ ee-mehl

Leisure

Sightseeing and tourist office
• •

The tourist office is sometimes called **le syndicat d'initiative**, but usually **l'office de/du tourisme**. Most museums are closed on Tuesdays. Like shops, some museums and other tourist attractions are closed between 12 and 2 p.m.

Where is the tourist office?	**Où est l'office de tourisme?** oo eh lo-fees duh too-reesm?
What is there to visit in the area?	**Qu'est-ce qu'il y a à voir dans la région?** kes keel ya a vwar dahñ la ray-zhyoñ?
Is it OK to take children?	**On peut y aller avec des enfants?** on puh ee a-lay a-vek day zahñ-fahñ?
Do you have any leaflets?	**Avez-vous de la documentation?** a-vay voo duh la do-kew-mahñ-ta-syoñ?

71

Are there any excursions?	**Est-ce qu'il y a des excursions?** es keel ya day zek-skewr-syoñ?
We'd like to go to...	**On voudrait aller à...** oñ voo-dreh a-lay a...
How much does it cost to get in?	**C'est combien l'entrée?** say koñ-byañ lahñ-tray?
Are there any reductions for...?	**Est-ce que vous faites des réductions pour...?** es kuh voo feht day ray-dewk-syoñ poor...?
children	**les enfants** lay zahñ-fahñ
students	**les étudiants** lay zay-tew-dyahñ
unemployed people	**les chômeurs** lay shoh-mur
senior citizens	**les retraités** lay ruh-treh-tay

Entertainment

. . . .

Check at the local tourist office for information about local events. Two major festivals in France are the Cannes Film Festival (**festival de Cannes**) and the Avignon Arts Festival (**festival d'Avignon**). You can also find listings on **www.franceguide.fr**.

What is there to do in the evenings?	**Qu'est-ce qu'on peut faire le soir?**	
	kes koñ puh fehr luh swar?	
Do you have a list of events for this month?	**Vous avez une liste des festivités pour ce mois-ci?**	
	Voo za-vay ewn leest day fes-tee-vee-tay poor suh mwa-see?	
Is there anything for children to do?	**Est-ce qu'il y a des choses à faire pour les enfants?**	
	es keel ya day shohz a fehr poor lay zahñ-fahñ?	

Nightlife

. . . .

Where can I go clubbing?	**Où est-ce que je peux aller en boîte?**	
	oo es kuh zhuh puh a-lay ahñ bwat?	
bar	**le bar**	bar
gay bar/club	**le bar gay/ la discothèque gay**	bar geh/ dees-koh-tek geh
gig	**le concert**	koñ-sehr
music festival	**le festival de musique**	fest-ee-val duh mew-zeek
nightclub	**la boîte de nuit**	bwat duh nwee
party	**la fête**	fet
pub	**le pub**	puhb

Out and about

• •

Where can I/we...?	**Où est-ce qu'on peut...?** oo es koñ puh...?
go fishing	**pêcher** peh-shay
go riding	**faire du cheval** fehr dew shuh-val
Are there any good beaches near here?	**Est-ce qu'il y a de bonnes plages près d'ici?** es keel ya duh bon plazh preh dee-see?
Is there a swimming pool?	**Est-ce qu'il y a une piscine?** es keel ya ewn pee-seen?
Can you visit ... in a wheelchair?	**On peut visiter ... en fauteuil roulant?** oñ puh vee-zee-tay ... ahñ foh-tuh-yuh roo-lahñ?
What's on at the cinema?	**Qu'est-ce qui passe au cinéma?** kes kee pas oh see-nay-ma?
What is on at the theatre/at the opera?	**Qu'est-ce qu'on joue au théâtre/à l'opéra?** kes koñ zhoo oh tay-atr/a lo-pay-ra?
I'd like two tickets...	**Je voudrais deux billets...** zhuh voo-dreh duh bee-yeh...

74

| for tonight | **pour ce soir** | poor suh swar |
| for tomorrow night | **pour demain soir** | poor duh-mañ swar |

If you would like to try a traditional French activity, how about a game of pétanque (**la pétanque**)? Played outdoors with metal boules on various surfaces, your aim is to get your team's boules as close as possible to a small wooden ball.

adventure centre	**le parc de loisirs**	park duh lwa-zeer
art gallery	**le musée d'art**	mew-zay dar
boat hire	**la location de bateaux**	lo-ka-syoñ duh ba-toh
camping	**le camping**	kahñ-peeng
museum	**le musée**	mew-zay
piercing	**le piercing**	peer-seeng
tattoo	**le tatouage**	ta-too-azh
theme park	**le parc d'attractions**	park dah-trak-syoñ
water park	**le parc aquatique**	park a-kwa-teek
zoo	**le zoo**	zoh

Leisure

baignade interdite ben-yad añ-tehr-deet	no swimming
interdiction de plonger añ-tehr-deek-syoñ duh ploñ-zhay	no diving

Leisure

Music

• •

folk	**le folk**	follk
hip-hop	**le hip-hop**	ee-pop
pop	**la pop**	pop
reggae	**le reggae**	reg-geh
rock	**le rock**	rock
techno	**la techno**	tek-no

Are there any good concerts on?	**Il y a de bons concerts en ce moment?** eel ya duh boñ koñ-sehr ahñ suh mo-mahñ?
Where can we hear some classical music/ some jazz?	**Où est-ce qu'on peut aller écouter de la musique classique/du jazz?** oo es koñ puh a-lay ay-koo-tay duh la mew-zeek kla-seek/dew jaz?

76

Sport

• • • • • • • • • • • • • • • • • •

cycling	**le vélo**	vay-lo
dancing	**la danse**	dahñs
kayaking	**le kayak**	ka-yak
rock climbing	**l'escalade** *f*	es-ka-lad
snowboarding	**le snowboard**	sno-bord
volleyball	**le volley(-ball)**	vol-eh(-boll)
water-skiing	**le ski nautique**	skee no-teek
windsurfing	**la planche à voile**	plahñsh a vwal

Where can I/ we...?	**Où est-ce qu'on peut...?** oo es koñ puh...?
play tennis	**jouer au tennis** zhoo-ay oh teh-nees
play golf	**jouer au golf** zhoo-ay oh golf
go swimming	**faire de la natation** fehr duh la na-ta-syoñ
go jogging	**faire du jogging** fehr dew jo-geeng
How much is it per hour?	**C'est combien l'heure?** say koñ-byañ lur?
Do you have to be a member?	**Est-ce qu'il faut être membre?** es keel foh (t)etr mahñbr?

Can we hire...?	**Est-ce qu'on peut louer...?**
	es koñ puh loo-ay...?
rackets	**des raquettes**
	day ra-ket
golf clubs	**des clubs de golf**
	day club duh golf
What sports do you play?	**Qu'est-ce que vous faites comme sports?**
	kes kuh voo fet kom spor?
I want to try...	**Je voudrais essayer...**
	zhuh voo-dreh eh-say-yay...
I've never done this before	**Je ne l'ai encore jamais fait**
	zhuh nuh lay ahñ-kor zha-may feh
I would like to hire skis	**Je voudrais louer des skis**
	zhuh voo-dreh loo-ay day skee
How much is a pass for...?	**C'est combien le forfait pour...?**
	say koñ-byañ luh for-feh poor...?
a day	**une journée**
	ewn zhoor-nay
a week	**une semaine**
	ewn suh-men
Have you ever skied before?	**Vous avez déjà fait du ski?**
	voo za-vay day-zha feh dew skee?
What is your shoe size?	**Quelle pointure faites-vous?**
	kel pwañ-tewr fet voo?

Walking

• •

Do you have a
guide to local
walks?

**Avez-vous un guide des
promenades dans la région?**
a-vay vooz uñ geed day prom-nad
dahñ la ray-zhyoñ?

How many
kilometres is
the walk?

**La promenade fait combien
de kilomètres?**
la prom-nad feh koñ-byañ duh
kee-lo-metr?

Leisure

79

Communications

Telephone and mobile

• •

International codes for French-speaking countries
are **00 33** (France), **00 32** (Belgium), **00 352**
(Luxembourg) and **00 41** (Switzerland). When
phoning the UK from France, dial **00 44**, plus the
UK number without the first **0**.

I'd like to make a phone call	**Je voudrais téléphoner** zhuh voo-dreh tay-lay-fo-nay
What's your mobile number?	**Quel est le numéro de votre portable?** kel eh luh new-may-ro duh votr por-tabl?
Can I use your mobile?	**Je peux emprunter votre portable?** zhuh puh ahñ-pruñ-tay votr por-tabl?
My mobile number is...	**Le numéro de mon portable est...** luh new-may-ro duh moñ por-tabl ay...

80

Do you have a ... charger/cable?	**Est-ce que vous avez un chargeur/un câble pour...?**
	es kuh voo za-vay uñ shar-zhur/ uñ kabl poor...?
Can I borrow your...?	**Est-ce que je peux vous emprunter votre...?**
	es kuh zhuh puh ahñ-pruñ-tay votr...?
smartphone	**le smartphone**
	smart-fon
I have an e-ticket on my phone	**J'ai un billet électronique sur mon téléphone**
	zhay uñ bee-yay ay-lek-tro-neek sewr moñ tay-lay-fon
I need to phone a UK/a US/an Australian number	**Je voudrais composer un numéro de téléphone au Royaume-Uni/aux États-Unis/en Australie**
	zhuh voo-dreh kom-po-zay uñ noo-may-roh duh tay-lay-fon oh rwa-yohm ew-nee/oh zay-ta-zew-nee/ahñ oh-stra-lee

FACE TO FACE

Âllo?
alo?
Hello

Bonjour. Je voudrais parler à..., s'il vous plaît
boñ-zhoor, zhuh voo-dreh par-lay a..., seel voo pleh
Hello, I'd like to speak to..., please

C'est de la part de qui?
say duh la par duh kee?
Who's calling?

De la part de...
duh la par duh...
This is...

Un instant, s'il vous plaît...
uñ nañ-stahñ seel voo pleh...
Just a moment...

Can I speak to...?	**Pourrais-je parler à...?** poo-rezh par-lay a...?
It's (your name)	**...à l'appareil** ...a la-pa-ray
How do I get an outside line?	**Comment on fait pour avoir une ligne extérieure?** ko-mahñ oñ feh poor a-vwar ewn leen-yuh ek-stay-ree-ur?
I'll call back...	**Je vous rappellerai...** zhuh voo ra-pel-ray...
later	**plus tard** plew tar
tomorrow	**demain** duh-mañ

Je vous le/la passe zhuh voo luh/la pas	I'm putting you through
C'est occupé say to-kew-pay	It's engaged
Pouvez-vous rappeler plus tard? poo-vay voo ra-play plew tar?	Can you call back later?
Voulez-vous laisser un message? voo-lay voo leh-say uñ meh-sazh?	Do you want to leave a message?
Veuillez laisser votre message après le bip sonore vuh-yay leh-say votr meh-sazh a-preh luh beep so-nor	Please leave a message after the tone
S'il vous plaît, éteignez votre portable seel voo pleh, ay-ten-yay votr por-tabl	Please turn your mobile off

Communications

83

Text messaging

text (message)	**le texto, le SMS** text-oh, es-em-es	
send a text (message)	**envoyer un texto/SMS** ahñ-vwa-yay uñ text-oh/es-em-es	
I will text you	**Je t'enverrai un texto/SMS** zhuh tahñ-veh-ray uñ text-oh/ es em es	
Can you text me?	**Tu peux m'envoyer un texto/SMS?** tew puh mahñ-vwa-yay uñ text-oh/es em es?	

A+	**à plus tard**	see you later
dac	**d'accord**	OK (in agreement)
2m1	**demain**	tomorrow
MDR	**mort de rire**	(equivalent of) LOL
jtm	**je t'aime**	I love you
pk?	**pourquoi**	why?
koi	**quoi**	what
stp	**s'il te plaît**	please

E-mail

· ·

What's your e-mail address?	**Quelle est votre adresse e-mail?** kel ay votr a-dres ee-mehl?
How do you spell it?	**Comment ça s'écrit?** ko-mahñ sa say-kree?
All one word	**En un seul mot** ahñ uñ suhl moh
My e-mail address is...	**Mon adresse e-mail est...** moñ nad-res ee-mehl ay...
caroline.smith@ bit.co.uk	**caroline point smith arobase bit point CO point UK** ka-roh-leen pwañ smeet a-roh-baz bit pwañ say oh pwañ ew ka
Can I send an e-mail?	**Je peux envoyer un e-mail?** zhuh puh ahñ-vwa-yay uñ nee-mehl?

Internet

accueil a-kuh-yuh	home
nom d'utilisateur noñ dew-tee-lee-za-tur	username
moteur de recherche mo-tur duh ruh-shehrsh	search engine
mot de passe moh duh pas	password
wifi wee-fee	Wi-Fi
réseau social ray-zoh so-syal	social network
appli ap-lee	app
ordinateur portable, portable (or-dee-na-tur) por-tabl	laptop
tablette tab-let	tablet

I can't log on	**Je n'arrive pas à me connecter** zhuh na-reev pa a muh ko-nek-tay
What is the Wi-Fi password?	**Quel est le mot de passe wifi?** kel ay luh moh duh pass wee-fee?

Do you have free Wi-Fi?	**Est-ce que vous avez le wifi gratuit?**
	es kuh voo za-vay luh wee-fee gra-twee?
Add me on Facebook	**Ajoutez-moi comme ami(e) sur Facebook**
	ah-zhoo-tay mwa kom a-mee sewr face-book
Is there a 3G/4G signal?	**Est-ce que vous avez le réseau 3G/4G?**
	es kuh voo za-vay luh ray-zoh trwa-zhay/katr zhay?
I need to access my webmail	**J'ai besoin d'accéder à mon webmail**
	zhay buh-zwañ dak-say-day a moñ web-mehl
I would like to use Skype	**J'aimerais utiliser Skype**
	zhem-uh-reh ew-tee-lee-zay skype

Practicalities

Money

. . . .

Banks are generally open from 9 a.m. to 4.30 p.m. Monday to Friday, but as closing times vary, you are best advised to go in the morning.

distributeur dees-tree-bew-tur	cash machine
les dollars do-lar	dollars
les livres (sterling) leevr ster-leeng	pounds
le taux de change toh duh shahñzh	exchange rate

Where can I change some money?	**Où est-ce que je peux changer de l'argent?** oo es kuh zhuh puh shahñ-zhay duh lar-zhahñ?
When does the bank open?	**La banque ouvre à quelle heure?** la bahñk oovr a kel ur?

When does the bank close?	**La banque ferme à quelle heure?**
	la bahñk fehrm a kel ur?
Can I pay with pounds/euros?	**Je peux payer en livres sterling/en euros?**
	zhuh puh pay-yay ahñ leevr stehr-leeng/ahñ nuh-roh?
Can I use my credit card in this cash machine?	**Je peux utiliser ma carte (de crédit) dans ce distributeur?**
	zhuh puh ew-tee-lee-zay ma kart (duh kray-dee) dahñ suh dee-stree-bew-tur?
Do you have any change?	**Vous avez de la monnaie?**
	voo za-vay duh la mo-neh?
What is the exchange rate for...?	**Quel est le taux de change de...?**
	kel ay luh toh duh shahñzh duh...?

Paying

· ·

l'addition la-dee-syoñ	bill (restaurant)
la note la not	bill (hotel)
la facture la fak-tewr	invoice
la caisse la kes	cash desk

paiement uniquement en espèces pay-mahñ oo-neek-mahñ ahñ nes-pes	cash only
retirer de l'argent ruh-tee-ray duh l'ar-zhahñ	to withdraw money
la carte de paiement à débit immédiat kart duh pay-mahñ a day-bee ee-may-dya	debit card
la carte de crédit kart duh cray-dee	credit card
le paiement sans contact pay-mahñ sahñ koñ-takt	contactless payment
la carte prépayée en devises kart pray-pay-ay ahñ duh-veez	prepaid currency card

How much is it?   **C'est combien?/Ça fait combien?**
say koñ-byañ/sa feh koñ-byañ?

Can I pay...?   **Je peux payer...?**
zhuh puh pay-yay...?

by credit card   **par carte de crédit**
par kart duh kray-dee

by cheque   **par chèque**
par shek

The bill, please (restaurant)	**L'addition, s'il vous plaît** la-dee-syoñ, seel voo pleh
Where do I pay?	**Où doit-on payer?** oo dwa-toñ pay-yay?
Is service included?	**Le service est compris?** luh sehr-vees ay koñ-pree?
Could you give me a receipt, please?	**Pourriez-vous me donner un reçu, s'il vous plaît?** poo-ree-ay voo muh do-nay uñ ruh-sew, seel voo pleh?
Do I pay in advance?	**Est-ce qu'il faut payer à l'avance?** es keel foh pay-yay a la-vahñs?
I've nothing smaller (no change)	**Je n'ai pas de monnaie** zhuh nay pa duh mo-neh
Can I pay in cash?	**Est-ce que je peux payer en espèces/en liquide?** es kuh zhuh puh pay-ay ahñ es- pes/ahñ lee-keed?
Where is the nearest cash machine?	**Où se trouve le distributeur le plus proche?** oo suh troov luh dees-tree-bew-tur luh plew prosh?
Is there a credit card charge?	**Est-ce qu'il y a des frais d'utilisation de la carte de crédit?** es keel ya day freh dew-tee-lee-za-syoñ duh la kart duh kray-dee?

Is there a discount for senior citizens/ children?	**Est-ce qu'il y a une réduction pour les personnes âgées/ les enfants?** es keel ya ewn ray-dewk-syoñ poor lay per-son za-zhay/lay zahñ-fahñ?
Can you write down the price?	**Pouvez-vous m'écrire le prix?** poo-vay voo may-kreer luh pree?

Luggage

. . . .

le retrait des bagages luh ruh-treh day ba-gazh	baggage reclaim
la consigne la koñ-see-nyuh	left luggage
le chariot à bagages luh sha-ryoh a ba-gazh	luggage trolley

My luggage hasn't arrived yet	**Mes bagages ne sont pas encore arrivés** may ba-gazh nuh soñ pa ahñ-kor a-ree-vay
My suitcase has been damaged on the flight	**Ma valise a été abîmée pendant le vol** ma va-leez a ay-tay a-bee-may pahñ-dahñ luh vol

Laundry

le pressing luh preh-seeng	dry-cleaner's
la laverie automatique la lav-ree oh-to-ma-teek	launderette
la lessive en poudre la leh-seev ahñ poodr	washing powder

Is there ... near here? **Est-ce qu'il y a ... près d'ici?**
es keel ya ... preh dee-see?

Complaints

This doesn't work	**Ça ne marche pas** sa nuh marsh pa
It's dirty	**C'est sale** say sal
The ... doesn't work	**Le/La ... ne marche pas** luh/la ... nuh marsh pa
light	**la lumière** la lew-myehr
lock	**la serrure** la seh-rewr

heating	**le chauffage** luh shoh-fazh
air conditioning	**la climatisation** la klee-ma-tee-za-syoñ
I want a refund	**Je veux être remboursé(e)** zhuh vuh etr rahñ-boor-say

Problems

• •

Can you help me?	**Pouvez-vous m'aider?** poo-vay voo meh-day?
I speak very little French	**Je parle très peu le français** zhuh parl treh puh luh frahñ-seh
Does anyone here speak English?	**Est-ce qu'il y a quelqu'un qui parle anglais ici?** es keel ya kel-kuñ kee parl ahñ-gleh ee-see?
I would like to speak to whoever is in charge	**Je voudrais parler au responsable** zhuh voo-dreh par-lay oh reh-spoñ-sabl
I'm lost	**Je me suis perdu(e)** zhuh muh swee pehr-dew
How do I get to...?	**Pour aller à/au...?** poor a-lay a/oh...?

I missed...	**J'ai raté...**
	zhay ra-tay...
my train	**mon train**
	moñ trañ
my plane	**mon avion**
	moñ na-vyoñ
my connection	**ma correspondance**
	ma ko-res-poñ-dahñs
The coach has left without me	**Le car est parti sans moi**
	luh kar ay par-tee sahñ mwa
Can you show me how this works?	**Pouvez-vous me montrer comment ça marche?**
	poo-vay voo muh moñ-tray ko-mahñ sa marsh?
I have lost my purse	**J'ai perdu mon porte-monnaie**
	zhay pehr-dew moñ port-mo-neh
I need to get to...	**Je dois aller à/au (etc.)...**
	zhuh dwa a-lay a/oh...
Leave me alone!	**Laissez-moi tranquille!**
	leh-say mwa trahñ-keel!
Go away!	**Allez-vous en!**
	a-lay voo zahñ!
the elderly	**les personnes âgées**
	pehr-son za-zhay
Where can I recycle this?	**Où est-ce que je peux recycler cela?**
	oo es kuh zhuh puh ruh-see-klay suh-la?

I need to access my online banking	**J'ai besoin d'accéder à mon compte bancaire en ligne** zhay buh-zwañ dak-say-day a moñ koñt bahñ-kehr oñ lee-nyuh
Do you have wheelchairs?	**Est-ce qu'il y a des fauteuils roulants?** es keel ya day foh-tuh-yuh roo-lahñ?
Do you have an induction loop?	**Est-ce que vous avez une boucle pour malentendants?** es kuh voo za-vay ewñ bookl poor mal-ahñ-tahñ-dahñ?
This is broken	**C'est cassé** say ka-say
Can you repair...?	**Pouvez-vous réparer...?** poo-vay voo ray-pa-ray...?

Emergencies

• •

In France, the emergency service phone numbers are as follows: the French ambulance and emergency service (called **SAMU**, Service d'aide médicale urgente) **15**, police **17**, fire brigade **18**.

police po-lees	police
ambulance ahñ-bew-lahñs	ambulance

pompiers poñ-pyay		fire brigade
commissariat ko-mee-sar-ya		police station (in large towns)
gendarmerie zhahñ-darm-ree		police station (in villages and small towns)
urgences ewr-zhahñs		accident and emergency department

Help!	**Au secours!** oh skoor!
Fire!	**Au feu!** oh fuh!
Can you help me?	**Pouvez-vous m'aider?** poo-vay voo meh-day?
There has been an accident	**Il y a eu un accident** eel ya ew uñ nak-see-dahñ
Someone has been injured	**Il y a un blessé** eel ya uñ bleh-say
Please call...	**S'il vous plaît, appelez...** seel voo pleh, a-puh-lay...
the police	**la police** la po-lees
an ambulance	**une ambulance** ewn ahñ-bew-lahñs
Where is the police station?	**Où est le commissariat?** oo eh luh ko-mee-sar-ya?
I want to report a theft	**Je veux signaler un vol** zhuh vuh seen-ya-lay uñ vol

I've been robbed/ attacked	**On m'a volé/attaqué(e)** oñ ma vo-lay/a-ta-kay
I've been raped	**On m'a violée** oñ ma vee-o-lay
I want to speak to a policewoman	**Je veux parler à une femme agent de police** zhuh vuh par-lay a ewn fam a-zhañ duh po-lees
Someone has stolen...	**On m'a volé...** oñ ma vo-lay...
my handbag	**mon sac à main** moñ sak a mañ
my money	**mon argent** moñ nar-zhahñ
My car has been broken into	**On a forcé ma voiture** oñ na for-say ma vwa-tewr
My car has been stolen	**On m'a volé ma voiture** oñ ma vo-lay ma vwa-tewr
I need to make a telephone call	**Il faut que je passe un coup de téléphone** eel foh kuh zhuh pas uñ koo duh tay-lay-fon
I need a report for my insurance	**Il me faut un constat pour mon assurance** eel muh foh uñ kon-sta poor moñ na-sew-rahñs

98

I didn't know the speed limit	**Je ne savais pas quelle était la limite de vitesse**
	zhuh nuh sa-veh pa kel ay-teh la lee-meet duh vee-tes
How much is the fine?	**C'est une amende de combien?**
	say tewn a-mahñd duh koñ-byañ?
Where do I pay it?	**Où dois-je la payer?**
	oo dwa-zhuh la pay-yay?

YOU MAY HEAR...

| **Vous avez brûlé un feu rouge** voo za-vay brew-lay uñ fuh roozh | You went through a red light |
| **Vous n'avez pas cédé la priorité** voo na-vay pa say-day la pree-o-ree-tay | You didn't give way |

If you are walking around large cities in France, especially Paris, be aware that drivers often feel no obligation to stop at pedestrian crossings unless there is a red light.

Health

Pharmacy

la pharmacie la far-ma-see	pharmacy/chemist's
la pharmacie de garde la far-ma-see duh gard	duty chemist's

Can you give me something for...?	**Avez-vous quelque chose contre...?** a-vay voo kel-kuh shohz koñtr...?
a headache	**le mal de tête** luh mal duh tet
car sickness	**le mal des transports** luh mal day trahñ-spor
flu	**la grippe** la greep
diarrhoea	**la diarrhée** la dya-ray
sunburn	**les coups de soleil** lay koo duh so-leh-yuh

| Is it safe for children? | **C'est sans danger pour les enfants?** say sahñ dahñ-zhay poor lay zahñ-fahñ? |
| How much should I give him/her? | **Combien dois-je lui en donner?** koñ-byañ dwa zhuh lwee ahñ do-nay? |

| **Prenez-en trois fois par jour avant/pendant/ après le repas** pruh-nay zahñ trwa fwa par zhoor avahñ/ pahñ-dahñ/a-preh luh ruh-pa | Take it three times a day before/with/after meals |

Health

asthma	**l'asthme** *m*	as-muh
condom	**le préservatif**	pray-zehr-va-teef
contact lenses	**les lentilles de contact**	lahñ-tee duh koñ-takt
inhaler	**l'inhalateur** *m*	een-a-la-tur
morning-after pill	**la pilule du lendemain**	pee-lewl dew lahñ-duh-mañ
mosquito bite	**la piqûre de moustique**	pee-kewr duh moo-steek
mosquito repellent	**la lotion anti-moustiques**	la lo-syoñ ahñ-tee-moos-teek

painkillers	**les analgésiques**	a-nal-zhay-zeek
period	**les règles**	reh-gluh
the Pill	**la pilule**	pee-lewl
tampon	**le tampon**	tahñpoñ

Doctor

. . . .

hôpital o-pee-tal	hospital
urgences ewr-zhahñst	accident and emergency department
consultations koñ-sewl-ta-syoñ	surgery hours

FACE TO FACE

Je me sens mal
zhuh muh sahñ mal
I feel ill

Vous avez de la fièvre?
voo za-vay duh la fyehvr?
Do you have a temperature?

Non, j'ai mal ici
noñ, zhay mal ee-see
No, I have a pain here

I need a doctor	**J'ai besoin d'un médecin**
	zhay buh-zwañ duñ may-dsañ
My son/My daughter is ill	**Mon fils/Ma fille est malade**
	moñ fees/ma fee ay ma-lad
I'm diabetic	**Je suis diabétique**
	zhuh swee dya-bay-teek
I'm pregnant	**Je suis enceinte**
	zhuh swee ahñ-sañt
I'm on the pill	**Je prends la pilule**
	zhuh prahñ la pee-lewl
I'm allergic to penicillin	**Je suis allergique à la pénicilline**
	zhuh swee za-lehr-zheek a la pay-nee-see-leen
How much will it cost?	**Combien ça va coûter?**
	koñ-byañ sa va koo-tay?
I need a receipt for the insurance	**Il me faut un reçu pour l'assurance**
	eel muh foh uñ ruh-sew poor la-sew-rahñs
I'm allergic...	**Je suis allergique...**
	zhuh swee za-lehr-zheek...
to pollen	**au pollen** oh pol-en
to dairy	**aux produits laitiers**
	oh pro-dwee leh-tyay
to gluten	**au gluten** oh glew-ten
to nuts	**aux fruits à coque** oh frwee a cok
I have a prescription for...	**J'ai une ordonnance pour...**
	zhay ewn or-doñ-ahñs poor...

I've run out of medication	**Je n'ai plus de médicaments**
	zhuh nay plew duh may-dee-ka-mahñ
epilepsy	**l'épilepsie** *f*
	ay-pee-lep-see
STI/STD (sexually transmitted infection/disease)	**l'IST** *f*/**la MST (infection/ maladie sexuellement transmissible)**
	ee-es-tay/em-es-tay (añ-fek-syoñ/ ma-la-dee sek-sew-el-mahñ trahñs-mee-seeble)
food poisoning	**l'intoxication alimentaire** *f*
	añ-tok-see-ka-syoñ a-lee-mahñ-tehr
drug abuse	**la toxicomanie**
	tok-see-ko-ma-nee
sprain	**l'entorse** *f*
	oñ-tors
GP (general practitioner)	**le(la) généraliste**
	zhay-nay-ra-leest
A&E (accident and emergency)	**les urgences**
	ewr-zhahñs

YOU MAY HEAR...	
Il faut que vous alliez à l'hôpital eel foh kuh voo zal-yay a lo-pee-tal	You will have to go to hospital
Ce n'est pas très grave suh nay pa treh grav	It's not serious

Ne consommez pas d'alcool nuh con-som-ay pa dal-kol	Do not drink alcohol
Est-ce que vous buvez? es kuh voo bew-vay?	Do you drink?
Est-ce que vous fumez? es kuh voo foo-may?	Do you smoke?
Est-ce que vous vous droguez? es kuh voo voo dro-gay?	Do you take drugs?

arm	**le bras**	bra
back	**le dos**	doh
chest	**la poitrine**	pwa-treen
ear	**l'oreille** *f*	or-ay-yuh
eye	**l'œil** *m*	uhy
foot	**le pied**	pyay
head	**la tête**	tet
heart	**le cœur**	kur
leg	**la jambe**	zhahñb
neck	**le cou**	koo
toe	**l'orteil** *m*	or-tay
tooth	**la dent**	dahñ
wrist	**le poignet**	pwa-nyay

Health

Dentist

· ·

I need to see a dentist	**J'ai besoin de voir un dentiste** zhay buh-zwañ duh vwar uñ dahñ-teest
He/She has toothache	**Il/Elle a mal aux dents** eel/el a mal oh dahñ
Can you do a temporary filling?	**Pouvez-vous me faire un plombage provisoire?** poo-vay voo muh fehr uñ ploñ-bazh pro-vee-zwar?
Can you give me something for the pain?	**Pouvez-vous me donner quelque chose contre la douleur?** poo-vay voo muh do-nay kel-kuh shohz koñtr la doo-lur?
a crown	**une couronne** ewn koo-ron
a wisdom tooth	**une dent de sagesse** ewn dahñ duh sazh-ess
It hurts	**Ça me fait mal** sa muh feh mal
Can you repair my dentures?	**Pouvez-vous me réparer mon dentier?** poo-vay voo muh ray-pa-ray moñ dahñt-yay?

Il faut l'arracher eel foh la-ra-shay	It has to come out
Il faut faire un plombage eel foh fehr uñ ploñ-bazh	You need a filling

Eating out

Eating places

Salon de thé Generally attached to a cake shop, **pâtisserie**, where you can sit down and sample some of the cakes. Can be quite expensive.

Crêperie Specialising in sweet (**crêpes**) and savoury (**galettes**) pancakes. Good for light, inexpensive meals.

Libre-service Self-service.

Bistro Small, often family-owned, restaurant serving traditional, reasonably priced food.

Glacier Ice-cream parlour.

Restaurant Generally open 11.30 a.m. to 2.30 p.m. and 7.30 to 10.30 p.m. The menu is posted outside.

Table d'hôte Home cooking using local produce.

Brasserie Large café that serves food and drink all day and usually late into the night.

Frites 500m Signals a roadside café 500 metres away. Mediocre food (mostly chips).

L'aire de pique-nique Picnic area.

In a bar/café

. . . .

If you just ask for **un café** you will be served a small, strong, black coffee.

un (café) crème uñ (ka-fay) kreml	milky coffee, similar to a latte
un café au lait uñ ka-fay oh leh	coffee with hot milk

a coffee	**un café** uñ ka-fay	
a decaf	**un déca** uñ day-ka	
an orangeade	**une orangeade** ewn o-rahñ-zhad	
with lemon	**au citron** oh see-troñ	
no sugar	**sans sucre** sahñ sewkr	
for me	**pour moi** poor mwa	
for him/her	**pour lui/elle** poor lwee/el	
with ice, please	**avec des glaçons, s'il vous plaît** a-vek day gla-soñ, seel voo pleh	

Some ... mineral water	De l'eau minérale... duh loh mee-nay-ral...
sparkling	**gazeuse** ga-zuhz
still	**plate** plat

FACE TO FACE

Qu'est-ce que vous prenez?
kes kuh voo pruh-nay?
What will you have?

Un thé au lait, s'il vous plaît
uñ tay oh leh, seel voo pleh
A tea with milk, please

Other drinks to try

un chocolat (chaud) hot chocolate

un citron pressé freshly-squeezed lemon (add water and sugar)

un diabolo lemonade and cordial

une infusion/une tisane herbal tea

Reading the menu

Restaurants display their menus outside.
Often there is a choice of two or three menus
at different prices as well as **à la carte** dishes.
It is advisable to book on Saturday evenings,
especially in small towns.

Boisson non comprise Drink not included.

Plat du jour à 7 € 50 Today's special 7 € 50

Menu – entrée + plat + café
Set menu – starter + main course + coffee.

carte	menu
entrées	starters
potages	soups
assiette de charcuterie	assorted cold meats
assiette de crudités	assorted raw veg and dip
viandes	meat
gibier et volaille	game and poultry
poissons	fish
fruits de mer	seafood
légumes	vegetables
fromages	cheese

desserts	desserts
boissons	drinks
fait(e) maison	homemade
spécialité régionale	local delicacy

In a restaurant

• •

French people usually dine around 8 p.m. In a
brasserie, you can have just one course if you
wish, but in a **restaurant** you normally have at
least two courses. As service is included in the bill,
French people do not leave huge tips: around
€2 for a €50 meal would be the norm.

FACE TO FACE

Je voudrais réserver une table pour ... personnes
zhuh voo-dreh ray-zehr-vay ewn tabl poor ... pehr-son
I'd like to book a table for ... people

Oui, pour quand?
wee, poor kahñ?
Yes, when for?

**Pour ce soir/pour demain soir/pour dix-neuf
heures trente**
poor suh swar/poor duh-mañ swar/poor deez-nuh vur
trahñt
For tonight/for tomorrow night/for 7.30

The menu, please	**La carte, s'il vous plaît** la kart, seel voo pleh
What is the dish of the day?	**Quel est le plat du jour?** kel eh luh pla dew zhoor?
I'll have the menu at ... euros, please	**Je prends le menu à ... euros, s'il vous plaît** zhuh prahñ luh muh-new a ... uh-roh, seel voo pleh
Can you recommend a local dish?	**Pouvez-vous nous recommander un plat régional?** poo-vay voo noo ruh-ko-mahñ-day uñ pla ray-zhyo-nal?
What is in this?	**Qu'est-ce qu'il y a dedans?** kes keel ya duh-dahñ?
I'll have this	**Je prends ça** zhuh prahñ sa
More bread...	**Encore du pain...** ahñ-kor dew pañ...
More water...	**Encore de l'eau...** ahñ-kor duh loh...
Do you have a children's menu?	**Est-ce que vous avez un menu enfant?** es kuh voo za-vay uñ muh-new ahñ-fahñ?
a high chair	**une chaise haute (pour enfants)** ewn shez ot (poor ahñ-fahñ)

The bill, please	**L'addition, s'il vous plaît**	
	la-dee-syoñ, seel voo pleh	
Is service included?	**Est-ce que le service est compris?**	
	es kuh luh sehr-vees ay koñ-pree?	
Is there a set menu?	**Est-ce que vous avez un menu?**	
	es kuh voo za-vay uñ muh-new?	
We would like a table for ... people please	**Une table pour ... personnes, s'il vous plaît**	
	ewn tabl poor ... per-son, seel voo play	
This isn't what I ordered	**Ce n'est pas ce que j'ai commandé**	
	suh nay pa suh kuh zhay ko-mahñ-day	
The ... is too...	**Le(la) ... est trop...**	
	Luh(la) ... ay troh...	

cold	**froid(e)**	frwa(d)
greasy	**gras(se)**	gra(s)
rare	**saignant(e)**	say-nyahñ(t)
salty	**salé(e)**	sa-lay
spicy	**épicé(e)**	ay-pee-say
warm	**chaud(e)**	shoh(d)
well cooked	**bien cuit(e)**	byañ kwee(t)

Dietary requirements

· ·

coeliac disease	la maladie cœliaque	ma-la-dee say-lyak
dairy	les produits laitiers	pro-dwee leh-tyay
gluten	le gluten	glew-ten
halal	halal	a-lal
nuts	les noix/les fruits à coque	nwa/frwee a cok
organic	bio	bee-yo
vegan	le(la) végétalien(ne)	vay-zhay-talyañ/ lyen
wheat	le blé	blay

I have a ... allergy	Je suis allergique au/à la/ aux... zhuh swee za-lehr-zheek oh/a-la/ oh...
Is it ...-free?	Est-ce que c'est sans...? es kuh say sahñ...?
I don't eat...	Je ne mange pas de... zhuh nuh mahñzh pa duh...
Are there any vegetarian restaurants here?	Est-ce qu'il y a des restaurants végétariens ici? es keel ya day res-toh-rahñ vay-zhay-ta-ryañ ee-see?

115

| Do you have any vegetarian dishes? | **Vous avez des plats végétariens?** voo za-vay day pla vay-zhay-ta-ryañ? |
| Is it made with vegetable stock? | **Est-ce que c'est fait avec du bouillon de légumes?** es kuh say feh a-vek dew boo-yoñ duh lay-gewm? |

Wines and spirits

● ●

The wine list, please	**La carte des vins, s'il vous plaît** la kart day vañ, seel voo pleh
white wine/ red wine	**du vin blanc/du vin rouge** dew vañ blahñ/dew vañ roozh
Can you recommend a good wine?	**Pouvez-vous nous recommander un bon vin?** poo-vay voo noo ruh-ko-mahñ-day uñ boñ vañ?
A bottle...	**Une bouteille...** ewn boo-tay-yuh...
A carafe...	**Un pichet...** uñ pee-sheh...
of the house wine	**de la cuvée du patron** duh la kew-vay dew pa-troñ

Wines

Beaujolais light, fruity wines (Burgundy)

Bordeaux region producing red (claret), rosé and dry and sweet white wines

Bourgueil light, fruity red wine to be drunk very young (Loire)

Chablis very dry, full-bodied white wine (Burgundy)

Champagne sparkling white/rosé (Champagne)

Châteauneuf-du-Pape good, full-bodied red wine (Rhône)

Cuvée vintage

Demi-sec medium dry (wine)

Gewürztraminer fruity, spicy white wine (Alsace)

Mousseux sparkling (wine)

Muscadet very dry white wine (Loire)

Premier cru first-class wine

Saint-Emilion good full-bodied red wine (Bordeaux)

Sancerre dry white wine (Loire)

Spirits and liqueurs

What liqueurs do you have?	**Qu'est-ce que vous avez comme digestifs?**
	kes kuh voo za-vay kom dee-zheh-steef?

Armagnac fine grape brandy from southwest France

Calvados apple brandy made from cider (Normandy)

Chartreuse aromatic herb liqueur made by Carthusian monks

Cognac high-quality white grape brandy

Cointreau orange-flavoured liqueur

Crème de cassis blackcurrant liqueur: *kir* white wine and cassis apéritif, *kir royal* champagne and cassis apéritif

Crème de menthe peppermint-flavoured liqueur

Eau de vie very strong brandy (often made from plum, pear, etc.)

Grand Marnier tawny-coloured, orange-flavoured liqueur

Kirsch cherry-flavoured spirit from Alsace

Marc white grape spirit

Mirabelle plum spirit from Alsace

Pastis aniseed-based apéritif (e.g. Pernod) to which water is added

Menu reader

à la/à l'/au/aux... in the style of.../with...
abats offal, giblets
aïoli rich garlic mayonnaise served on the side
and giving its name to the dish it accompanies:
cold steamed fish and vegetables
amuse-bouche nibbles
anchoïade anchovy paste usually served on grilled
French bread
andouille (eaten cold), **andouillette** (eaten hot)
spicy tripe sausage
arachide peanut (raw)
araignée de mer spider crab
armoricaine, à l' cooked with brandy, wine,
tomatoes and onions
aspic de volaille chicken in aspic
assiette dish, platter
assiette anglaise plate of assorted cold meats
assiette de charcuterie plate of assorted pâtés
and salami
assiette de crudités selection of raw vegetables
assiette du pêcheur assorted fish or seafood
baba au rhum rum baba
Badoit mineral water, very slightly sparkling

baekenofe stew of pork, mutton and beef slow-cooked in white wine with a sliced-potato topping (from Alsace)

bavarois moulded cream and custard pudding, usually served with fruit

Béarnaise, à la served with a sauce similar to mayonnaise but flavoured with tarragon and white wine

beignets fritters, doughnuts

beurre blanc, au served with a creamy sauce made of butter, white wine and shallots

bien cuit well done

bière beer

(bière) pression draught beer

bière blonde lager

bière brune bitter

bio(logique) organic

bis wholemeal (of bread or flour)

biscuit de Savoie sponge cake

bisque smooth, rich seafood soup

blanquette stew made from white meat such as veal or chicken, in a creamy white sauce

blanquette de veau veal stew in white sauce

blanquette de volaille chicken stew in white sauce

blette Swiss chard

bleu *(adjective)* very rare

bleu *(noun)* blue cheese

bœuf bourguignon beef in burgundy, onions and mushrooms

120

bœuf en daube rich beef stew with wine, olives, tomatoes and herbs

bombe glacée moulded ice-cream dessert

bouchée vol-au-vent

bouchée à la reine vol-au-vent filled with chicken or veal and mushrooms in a white sauce

boudin pudding made with offal and blood

boudin blanc white pudding

bouillabaisse rich seafood dish flavoured with saffron, originally from Marseilles

boulettes meatballs

brandade de morue dried salt cod puréed with potatoes and olive oil

brioche sweet bun

brioche aux fruits sweet bun with glacé fruit

brochette kebab

brochette, en on a skewer

bugnes doughnuts from the Lyons area

cabillaud fresh cod

café au lait coffee with hot milk

café gourmand coffee served with a selection of small desserts (such as a **macaron**, a mini **crème brûlée** and a mini chocolate cake, for example)

calisson sweet made from a paste of almonds and candied fruit

canard périgourdin roast duck with prunes, **pâté de foie gras** and truffles

caneton duckling

carbonnade de bœuf braised beef

cari curry

carottes Vichy carrots cooked in butter and sugar
carpe farcie carp stuffed with mushrooms or
foie gras
carte des vins wine list
cassoulet bean stew with pork or mutton, confit
duck and sausages (there are many regional variations)
caviar blanc mullet roe
caviar niçois paste made with anchovies and
olive oil
céleri rémoulade celeriac in a creamy mustard
and herb dressing
cèpes porcini mushrooms
cervelas smoked pork sausage, saveloy
cervelle brains (usually lamb or calf)
cervelle de Canut cheese dip made of **fromage
frais**, goat's cheese, herbs and white wine
champignons à la grecque mushrooms cooked in
wine, olive oil, herbs and tomato
champignons de Paris button mushrooms
chantilly slightly sweetened whipped cream
charlotte dessert made in a mould lined with
sponge fingers and filled with custard and/or fruit
chasseur literally hunter-style, cooked with white
wine, shallots, mushrooms and herbs
châteaubriand thick fillet steak
chaud(e) hot
chauffé(e) heated
chausson pasty filled with meat or seafood
chausson aux pommes apple turnover
122 **chichi** yum-yum (doughnut)

chocolat chaud hot chocolate

choucroute sauerkraut

choucroute garnie sauerkraut served with various types of sausages

cidre cider

citron pressé freshly squeezed lemon juice with water and sugar

civet thick stew

civet de langouste crayfish in wine sauce

civet de lièvre hare stewed in wine, onions and mushrooms

clafoutis baked dessert made from cherries in batter

clou de girofle clove

compote de fruits stewed fruit

confit pieces of meat preserved in fat

confit de canard/d'oie duck/goose meat preserved in its own fat

confiture d'orange marmalade

consommé clear soup, generally made from meat or fish stock

contre-filet sirloin steak

coq au vin chicken and mushrooms cooked in red wine

coquilles Saint-Jacques scallops

côtelettes d'agneau lamb cutlets

côtes de porc pork chops

cotriade fish stew (Brittany)

coulibiac salmon cooked in puff pastry

coulis puréed fruit sauce

coupe ice cream served in a dessert glass

crémant sparkling wine

crème anglaise fresh custard

crème au beurre butter cream with egg yolks and sugar

crème de cream of... (soup)

crème d'Argenteuil white asparagus soup

crème de cresson watercress soup

crème de marrons chestnut purée

crème pâtissière thick fresh custard used in tarts and desserts

crème renversée (or **crème caramel**) custard with a caramelised top

crêpes sweet and savoury pancakes

crêpes fourrées filled pancakes

crêpes Suzette pancakes in a Cointreau or Grand Marnier sauce, usually flambéed

crevette prawn

crevette grise shrimp

crevette rose large prawn

croque-madame grilled gruyère cheese and ham sandwich with a fried egg on top

croque-monsieur grilled gruyère cheese and ham sandwich

croûte, en in pastry

croûtons, aux served with croutons (cubes of toasted or fried bread)

cru(e) raw

crudités assortment of raw vegetables (grated carrots, sliced tomatoes, etc.) served as a starter

cuisses de grenouille frogs' legs

cuit cooked

daube casserole of beef with wine, herbs, garlic, tomatoes and olives

dauphinoise, à la baked in milk

daurade sea bream

diabolo soft drink of cordial and lemonade

eau de Seltz soda water

eau-de-vie brandy (often made from plum, pear, etc)

eau du robinet tap water

eau minérale mineral water

échine loin of pork

écrevisse freshwater crayfish

entrées starters

escargots snails (generally cooked with strong seasonings)

estouffade de boeuf beef stew cooked in red wine, herbs, onions, mushrooms and diced bacon

farci(e) stuffed

feu de bois, au cooked over a wood fire

feuille leaf

feuilleté(e) in puff pastry

filet de bœuf beef fillet

filet de bœuf en croûte beef Wellington

filet mignon small pork fillet steak

fine de claire high-quality oyster

fines herbes mixed, chopped herbs

flageolet type of small green haricot bean

florentine prepared with spinach, usually in a cheese sauce

foie liver (usually calf's)

foie de volaille chicken livers

foie gras goose liver

fond d'artichaut artichoke heart

fondue (au fromage) melted cheeses with white wine into which chunks of bread are dipped

fondue bourguignonne small chunks of beef dipped into boiling oil and eaten with different sauces

fougasse type of bread with various fillings (olives, anchovies)

four, au baked

fourré(e) stuffed

frais (fraîche) fresh

fraises des bois wild strawberries

frappé iced

fricassée stew of meat, usually chicken or veal, and vegetables

frit(e) fried

friture fried food, usually small fish

froid(e) cold

fromage blanc soft white cheese

fromage frais creamy fresh cheese

fumé(e) smoked

galantine meat in aspic

galette savoury buckwheat pancake

gambas large prawn

ganache chocolate cream filling

garni(e) garnished i.e. served with something, usually vegetables

garnitures side dishes

gâteau Saint-Honoré choux pastry cake filled with custard

gaufres waffles (often cream-filled)

gazeuse sparkling

gelée jelly, aspic

génoise sponge cake

germes de soja bean sprouts

gibier game

gigot d'agneau leg of lamb

gigot de mer large fish baked whole

gougère choux pastry with cheese

gratin, au topped with cheese and breadcrumbs and grilled

gratin dauphinois potatoes cooked in cream, garlic and Swiss cheese

grecque, à la cooked in olive oil, garlic, tomatoes and herbs, can be served hot or cold

grillade grilled meat

hachis mince

haricots beurre butter beans

haricots blancs haricot beans

haricots rouges red kidney beans

haricots verts green beans, French beans

hollandaise, sauce sauce made of butter, egg yolks and lemon juice, served warm

homard à l'armoricaine lobster cooked with onions, tomatoes and wine

hors-d'œuvre variés selection of appetizers

huile d'arachide groundnut oil

huile de tournesol sunflower oil

île flottante soft meringue floating on fresh custard

jambon de Bayonne cured raw ham from the Basque country

jambon de Paris boiled ham

julienne with vegetables cut into fine strips

jus juice; meat-based glaze or sauce

lait (demi-)écrémé (semi-)skimmed milk

lait entier full-cream milk

lamproie à la bordelaise lamprey in red wine

langouste crayfish (saltwater)

langoustines scampi (large)

langue tongue (veal, beef)

lard fat, streaky bacon

lardon strip of fat, diced bacon

loup de mer sea bass

macaron macaroon

macédoine (de fruits) fresh fruit salad

macédoine de légumes cooked mixed vegetables

madeleine small sponge cake

magret de canard duck breast

marcassin young wild boar

marinière, à la in a sauce of white wine, onions and herbs (mussels or clams)

marjolaine marjoram

marrons glacés candied chestnuts

marrons Mont Blanc chestnut purée and cream

matelote fresh-fish stew

128 **médaillon** medallion, small, round, thick slice of meat

merguez spicy red sausage

merlan whiting

merveilles fritters flavoured with brandy

mignonnette small fillet of lamb

mijoté(e) stewed

mille-feuille thin layers of pastry filled with custard

mirabelle small yellow plum; plum brandy from Alsace

mont-blanc pudding made with chestnuts and cream

Mornay, sauce béchamel and cheese sauce

morue dried salt cod

moules marinières mussels cooked in white wine

mousseline mashed potatoes with cream and eggs

noisettes d'agneau small round pieces of lamb

œufs à la coque soft-boiled eggs

œufs au plat fried eggs

œufs brouillés scrambled eggs

œufs durs hard-boiled eggs

œufs en cocotte eggs baked in individual containers with wine

œufs frits fried eggs

omelette nature plain omelette

omelette norvégienne baked Alaska

onglet hanger steak

pain au chocolat croissant with chocolate filling

pain bis brown bread

pain complet wholemeal bread

pain de mie white sliced loaf

pain d'épices ginger cake

pain de seigle rye bread
pain grillé toast
palmier caramelized puff pastry
pan bagnat bread roll with egg, olives, salad, tuna, anchovies and olive oil
pané(e) with breadcrumbs
panisse thick chickpea flour pancake
papillotes, en cooked in a paper or foil parcel
paris-brest ring-shaped cake filled with praline-flavoured cream
parisienne, à la sautéed in butter with white wine sauce and shallots
parmentier with potatoes
pâté de foie de volaille chicken liver pâté
pâté en croûte pâté encased in pastry
paupiettes slices of meat stuffed and rolled
pavé thick slice
Périgueux, sauce white wine sauce with truffles
persillé(e) with parsley
pétillant(e) fizzy
petit-beurre butter biscuit
petit pain roll
petits farcis stuffed tomatoes, aubergines, courgettes and peppers
petits fours bite-sized cakes and pastries
petit-suisse thick fromage frais
pilon drumstick (chicken)
piment doux sweet pepper
pimenté(e) peppery, hot
piment fort chilli

piperade tomato, pepper and onion stew, mixed with egg

pissaladière a kind of pizza made mainly in the Nice region, topped with onions, anchovies and black olives

pistou garlic, basil and olive oil sauce from Provence – similar to pesto

plat dish

plat (principal) main course

poché(e) poached

poêlé(e) pan-fried

point, à medium rare

poires belle Hélène poached pears with vanilla ice cream and chocolate sauce

pois cassés split peas

poitrine breast (lamb or veal)

pommes à l'anglaise boiled potatoes

pommes allumettes matchstick chips

pommes dauphine potato croquettes

pommes de terre à la lyonnaise potatoes fried with onions

pommes duchesse mashed potato piped into shapes then baked in the oven

pommes frites fried potatoes

pommes mousseline potatoes mashed with cream

pommes rissolées small deep-fried potatoes

pommes vapeur steamed potatoes

potage soup, generally creamed or thickened

pot-au-feu beef and vegetable stew

potée auvergnate cabbage and meat soup
potiron type of pumpkin
poularde fattened chicken
poulet basquaise chicken stew with tomatoes, mushrooms and peppers
poulet célestine chicken cooked in white wine with mushrooms and onion
poulpe à la niçoise octopus in tomato sauce
pousses de soja bean sprouts
poussin baby chicken
poutargue mullet roe paste
praliné hazelnut-flavoured
primeurs spring vegetables
provençale, à la cooked with tomatoes, peppers, garlic and white wine
pruneau prune, damson
purée mashed potatoes; purée
quatre-quarts cake made with equal parts of butter, flour, sugar and eggs
quenelles poached balls of fish or meat mousse served in a sauce
quenelles de brochet pike mousse in cream sauce
queue de bœuf oxtail
ragoût stew, casserole
raïto red wine, olive, caper, garlic and shallot sauce
râpé(e) grated
ratatouille tomatoes, aubergines, courgettes and garlic cooked in olive oil
rillettes coarse pork pâté

rillettes de canard coarse duck pâté

ris de veau calf sweetbread
rognons blancs testicles
rond de gigot lamb leg steak
rosbif roast beef
rôti(e) roast
rouille spicy version of garlic mayonnaise (**aïoli**)
served with fish stew or soup
roulade meat or fish, stuffed and rolled
roulé sweet or savoury roll
sabayon dessert made with egg yolks, sugar and
Marsala wine
sablé shortbread
saignant rare
salade de fruits fruit salad
salade de saison mixed salad and/or greens in
season
salade lyonnaise warm bacon and egg salad
salade niçoise many variations on a famous
theme: the basic ingredients are green beans,
anchovies, black olives and green peppers
salade russe cooked mixed vegetables in
mayonnaise
salade verte green salad
salé(e) salted; spicy
salsifis salsify (root vegetable resembling asparagus)
sanglier wild boar
sarriette savoury (herb)
sauce piquante sauce made from gherkins,
vinegar and shallots
saumon fumé smoked salmon

saumon poché poached salmon

sauté(e) sautéed

sauté d'agneau lamb stew

savarin filled ring-shaped cake

savoyarde, à la with gruyère cheese

sec dry; dried

selle d'agneau saddle of lamb

semoule semolina

sole meunière sole coated in flour, pan fried in butter and then served with the leftover butter as a sauce with parsley and lemon

sole Normande sole cooked in a cream, cider and shrimp sauce

sole Saint Germain grilled sole with butter and tarragon sauce

soufflé au Grand Marnier soufflé flavoured with Grand Marnier liqueur

soufflé au jambon ham soufflé

soupe à l'oignon onion soup usually served with a crisp slice of baguette in the dish with grated cheese piled on top

soupe au pistou vegetable soup with garlic and basil

soupe aux choux cabbage soup with pork

steak au poivre steak with peppercorns

sucré(e) sweet

suprême de volaille breast of chicken in cream sauce

tapenade olive paste

tarte open tart, generally sweet

tarte flambée thin pizza-like pastry topped with onion, cream and bacon (Alsace)

tarte normande apple tart

tarte tatin upside down tart with caramelized apples or pears

tarte tropézienne sponge cake filled with custard cream and topped with almonds

tartine open sandwich

terrine terrine, pâté

terrine de campagne pork and liver terrine

terrine de porc et gibier pork and game terrine

tête de veau calf's head

thé au citron tea with lemon

thé au lait tea with milk

thé sans sucre tea without sugar

thermidor grilled in its shell with cream sauce (lobster)

timbale round dish in which a mixture of meat or fish is cooked – often lined with pastry and served with a rich sauce

timbale d'écrevisses crayfish in a cream, wine and brandy sauce

timbale de fruits pastry base covered with fruits

tomates à la provençale tomatoes covered in breadcrumbs and garlic and baked

tomme type of cheese

tournedos thick fillet steak

tourte à la viande meat pie usually made with veal and pork

tripes à la mode de Caen tripe cooked with vegetables, herbs, cider and calvados

truite aux amandes trout cooked whole and garnished with almonds

vacherin large meringue filled with cream, ice cream and fruit

vapeur, à la steamed

veau sauté Marengo veal stewed with white wine, garlic, tomatoes and mushrooms

velouté thick creamy white sauce made with fish, veal or chicken stock; cream soup

verdure, en garnished with green vegetables

verjus juice of unripe grapes

verveine herbal tea made with verbena

viande séchée thin slices of cured meat

vichyssoise leek and potato soup, served cold

vin blanc white wine

vin de pays local regional wine

vin de table table wine

vin rosé rosé wine

vin rouge red wine

yaourt yoghurt

Reference

Alphabet

The French alphabet is the same as the English alphabet. Below are the words used for clarification when spelling something out.

Comment ça s'écrit? ko-mahñ sa say-kree?	How do you spell it?
A comme Anatole, B comme Berthe a kom a-na-tol, bay kom behrt	A for Anatole, B for Berthe

A	a	**Anatole**	a-na-tol
B	bay	**Berthe**	behrt
C	say	**Célestin**	say-les-tañ
D	day	**Désiré**	day-zee-ray
E	uh	**Eugène**	uh-zhen
F	ef	**François**	frahñ-swa
G	zhay	**Gaston**	gas-toñ
H	ash	**Henri**	ahñ-ree

I	ee	**Irma**	eer-ma
J	zhee	**Joseph**	zho-zef
K	ka	**Kléber**	klay-behr
L	el	**Louis**	loo-wee
M	em	**Marcel**	mar-sel
N	en	**Nicolas**	nee-koh-la
O	oh	**Oscar**	os-kar
P	pay	**Pierre**	pyehr
Q	kew	**Quentin**	kañ-tañ
R	ehr	**Raoul**	ra-ool
S	es	**Suzanne**	sew-zan
T	tay	**Thérèse**	tay-rez
U	ew	**Ursule**	ewr-sewl
V	vay	**Victor**	veek-tor
W	doo-bluh-vay	**William**	weel-yam
X	eex	**Xavier**	za-vyay
Y	ee-grek	**Yvonne**	ee-von
Z	zed	**Zoé**	zoh-ay

Measurements and quantities

• •

1 lb = approx. 0.5 kilo
1 pint = approx. 0.5 litre

Liquids

1/2 litre of...	**un demi-litre de...**
	uñ duh-mee leetr duh...
a litre of...	**un litre de...**
	uñ leetr duh...
1/2 bottle of...	**une demi-bouteille de...**
	ewn duh-mee-boo-tay-yuh duh...
a bottle of...	**une bouteille de...**
	ewn boo-tay-yuh duh...
a glass of...	**un verre de...**
	uñ vehr duh...

Weights

100 grams of...	**cent grammes de...**
	sahñ gram duh...
a kilo of...	**un kilo de...**
	uñ kee-loh duh...

Food

a slice of...	**une tranche de...**
	ewn trahñsh duh...
a portion of...	**une portion de...**
	ewn por-syoñ de...
a dozen...	**une douzaine de...**
	ewn doo-zen duh...

a box of...	**une boîte de...** ewn bwat duh...
a packet of...	**un paquet de...** uñ pa-keh duh...
a tin of...	**une boîte de...** ewn bwat duh...
a carton of...	**une brique de...** ewn breek duh...
a jar of...	**un pot de...** uñ poh duh...

Miscellaneous

a quarter	**un quart** uñ kar
ten per cent	**dix pour cent** dee poor sahñ
more...	**plus de...** plew duh...
less...	**moins de...** mwañ duh...
enough (of)...	**assez (de)...** a-say (duh)...
double	**le double** luh doobl
twice	**deux fois** duh fwa

Numbers

. . . .

0	**zéro** zay-roh
1	**un** uñ
2	**deux** duh
3	**trois** trwa
4	**quatre** katr
5	**cinq** sañk
6	**six** sees
7	**sept** set
8	**huit** weet
9	**neuf** nuhf
10	**dix** dees
11	**onze** oñz
12	**douze** dooz
13	**treize** trez
14	**quatorze** ka-torz
15	**quinze** kañz
16	**seize** sez
17	**dix-sept** dees-set
18	**dix-huit** deez-weet
19	**dix-neuf** deez-nuhf
20	**vingt** vañ
21	**vingt et un** vañ tay uñ
22	**vingt-deux** vañt-duh
23	**vingt-trois** vañt-trwa
30	**trente** trahñt
40	**quarante** ka-rahñt
50	**cinquante** sañk-ahñt
60	**soixante** swa-sahñt
70	**soixante-dix** swa-sahñt-dees

Reference

71	**soixante et onze**	swa-sahñt-ay-oñz
72	**soixante-douze**	swa-sahñt-dooz
80	**quatre-vingts**	katr-vañ
81	**quatre-vingt-un**	katr-vañ-un
82	**quatre-vingt-deux**	katr-vañ-duh
90	**quatre-vingt-dix**	katr-vañ-dees
91	**quatre-vingt-onze**	katr-vañ-oñz
100	**cent**	sahñ
110	**cent dix**	sahñ dees
200	**deux cents**	duh sahñ
250	**deux cent cinquante**	duh sahñ sañk-ahñt
1,000	**mille**	meel
1 million	**un million**	uñ mee-lyoñ

Days and months

• •

1st	**premier/première/ 1er/1ère**	pruh-myay/ pruh-myehr
2nd	**deuxième/2e**	duh-zyem
3rd	**troisième/3e**	trwa-zyem
4th	**quatrième/4e**	kat-ree-yem
5th	**cinquième/5e**	sañk-yem
6th	**sixième/6e**	see-zyem
7th	**septième/7e**	set-yem
8th	**huitième/8e**	wee-tyem
9th	**neuvième/9e**	nuh-vyem
10th	**dixième/10e**	dee-zyem

Days

Monday	**lundi**	luñ-dee
Tuesday	**mardi**	mar-dee
Wednesday	**mercredi**	mehr-kruh-dee
Thursday	**jeudi**	zhuh-dee
Friday	**vendredi**	vahñ-druh-dee
Saturday	**samedi**	sam-dee
Sunday	**dimanche**	dee-mahñsh

Months

January	**janvier**	zhahñ-vyay
February	**février**	fay-vree-yay
March	**mars**	mars
April	**avril**	av-reel
May	**mai**	meh
June	**juin**	zhwañ
July	**juillet**	zhwee-yeh
August	**août**	oo(t)
September	**septembre**	sep-tahñbr
October	**octobre**	ok-tobr
November	**novembre**	no-vahñbr
December	**décembre**	day-sahñbr

Seasons

spring	**printemps**	prañ-tahñ
summer	**été**	ay-tay
autumn	**automne**	oh-ton
winter	**hiver**	ee-vehr

What is today's date?	**Quel jour sommes-nous?** kel zhoor som noo?
It's the fifth of March	**Nous sommes le cinq mars** noo som luh sañk mars
It's 8th May 2016	**Nous sommes le huit mai deux mille seize** noo som luh wee may duh meel sez
1st January	**Le premier janvier** luh pruhm-yay zhahñ-vyay
on Saturday	**samedi** sam-dee
on Saturdays	**le samedi** luh sam-dee
every Saturday	**tous les samedis** too lay sam-dee
this Saturday	**ce samedi** suh sam-dee
next Saturday	**samedi prochain** sam-dee pro-shañ
at the beginning of June	**début juin** day-bew zhwañ

at the end of June	**fin juin** fañ zhwañ
before the summer	**avant l'été** a-vahñ lay-tay
during the summer	**pendant l'été** pahñ-dahñ lay-tay
after the summer	**après l'été** a-preh lay-tay

Time

. . . .

The 24-hour clock is used a lot more in Europe than in Britain. After 12.00 (midday), it continues: 13.00 (**treize heures** – one o'clock in the afternoon), 14.00 (**quatorze heures** – two o'clock), 15.00 (**quinze heures** – three o'clock), etc. until 24.00 (**vingt-quatre heures** – midnight). With the 24-hour clock, the words **quart** (quarter) and **demie** (half) aren't used:

13.15 (1.15 p.m.)	**treize heures quinze**
19.30 (7.30 p.m.)	**dix-neuf heures trente**
22.45 (10.45 p.m.)	**vingt-deux heures quarante-cinq**
What time is it?	**Il est quelle heure?/** **Quelle heure est-il?** eel ay kel ur?/kel ur ay-teel?

It's...	**Il est...**
	eel ay...
two o'clock	**deux heures**
	duh zur
three o'clock	**trois heures**
	trwa zur
six o'clock (etc.)	**six heures**
	see zur
It's one o'clock	**Il est une heure**
	eel ay (t)ewn ur
It's midday	**Il est midi**
	eel ay mee-dee
It's midnight	**Il est minuit**
	eel ay mee-nwee
9	**neuf heures**
	nuh vur
9.10	**neuf heures dix**
	nuh vur dees
quarter past 9	**neuf heures et quart**
	nuh vur ay kar
9.20	**neuf heures vingt**
	nuh vur vañ
9.30	**neuf heures et demie/**
	neuf heures trente
	nuh vur ay duh-mee/
	nuh vur trahñt
9.35	**dix heures moins vingt-cinq**
	dee zur mwañ vañt-sañk

quarter to 10	**dix heures moins le quart**
	dee zur mwañ luh kar
10 to 10	**dix heures moins dix**
	dee zur mwañ dees

Time phrases

• •

When does it...?	**Ça ... à quelle heure?**
	sa ... a kel ur?
open/close/ begin/finish	**ouvre/ferme/commence/ finit**
	oovr/fehrm/ko-mahñs/fee-nee
at three o'clock	**à trois heures**
	a trwa zur
before three o'clock	**avant trois heures**
	a-vahñ trwa zur
after three o'clock	**après trois heures**
	a-preh trwa zur
today	**aujourd'hui**
	oh-zhoor-dwee
tonight	**ce soir**
	suh swar
tomorrow	**demain**
	duh-mañ
yesterday	**hier**
	ee-yehr

Public holidays

When a public holiday falls on a Tuesday or Thursday, it is common for people to take the Monday or the Friday off as well. This is known as **faire le pont** (making a bridge). Many of the larger shops now open on public holidays, but it is always best to check before you go.

January 1st	**Le jour de l'An** New Year's Day	
March or April	**Le Lundi de Pâques** Easter Monday	
May 1st	**La Fête du Travail** Labour Day/May Day	
May 8th	**Le 8 mai** Victory Day	
April or May	**L'Ascension** The Ascension	
May or June	**Le Lundi de Pentecôte** Whit Monday (no longer an official holiday, but many employees are still given the day off)	
July 14th	**La Fête Nationale/ le 14 juillet** Bastille Day	
August 15th	**L'Assomption** The Assumption	
November 1st	**La Toussaint** All Saints' Day	
November 11th	**L'Armistice de 1918** Armistice Day	
December 25th	**Noël** Christmas Day	

Reference

Phonetic map

When travelling in France, you will need to bear in mind that place names as we know them are not necessarily the same in French. Imagine if you wanted to buy tickets at a train station but couldn't see your destination on the departures list! This handy map eliminates such problems by indicating the locations and local pronunciations of major towns and cities.

149

Grammar

Nouns

. . . .

Unlike English nouns, French nouns have a gender:
they are either masculine (**le**) or feminine (**la**).
Therefore words for *the* and *a(n)* must agree with
the noun they accompany. Like English nouns, they
can be singular or plural, but the plural words for
the (**les**) and *some* (**des**) are the same in both
masculine and feminine:

	masculine	feminine	plural
the	**le chat**	la rue	**les chats/ rues**
a, an	**un chat**	une rue	**des chats/ rues**

If the noun begins with a vowel (*a, e, i, o* or *u*) or,
sometimes, an *h*, **le** and **la** shorten to **l'**, e.g.
l'avion *(m)*, **l'école** *(f)*, **l'hôtel** *(m)*. The letter *h* is
never sounded in French and, unfortunately, there
is no rule for distinguishing which words beginning
with *h* take **l'** and which **le/la**.

Note: **le** and **les** used after the prepositions **à** (to, at) and **de** (any, some, of) contract as follows:

à + **le** = **au** (**au cinéma** but **à** <u>la</u> **gare**)

à + **les** = **aux** (**aux magasins** – applies to both *m* and *f*)

de + **le** = **du** (**du pain** but **de** <u>la</u> **confiture**)

de + **les** = **des** (<u>des</u> **pommes** – applies to both *m* and *f*)

Plurals

. . . .

The general rule is to add an **s** to the singular:

le chat → **les chats**

Exceptions occur with the following noun endings:
-eau, **-eu**, **-al**

le bat<u>eau</u> → **les bat<u>eaux</u>**
le nev<u>eu</u> → **les nev<u>eux</u>**
le chev<u>al</u> → **les chev<u>aux</u>**

Nouns ending in **s**, **x**, or **z** do not change in the plural.

le dos → **les dos**
le prix → **les prix**
le nez → **les nez**

Adjectives

• •

Adjectives normally follow the noun they describe in French, e.g:

la pomme <u>verte</u> → (the <u>green</u> apple)

French adjectives have to reflect the gender of the noun they describe. To make an adjective feminine, an **e** is added to the masculine form (where this does not already end in an **e**, e.g. **jeune**). A final consonant, which is usually silent in the masculine form, is pronounced in the feminine:

masculine	feminine
le livre vert (the green book) luh leevr vehr	**la pomme verte** (the green apple) la pom vehrt

To make an adjective plural, an **s** is added to the singular form: masculine plural – **verts** (remember the ending is still silent: vehr) or feminine plural – **vertes** (because of the **s**, the **t** is sounded: vehrt).

My, your, his, her, their...

• •

These words also depend on the gender and number of the noun they accompany and not on the sex of the 'owner'.

	with masc. sing. noun	with fem. sing. noun	with plural noun
my	mon	ma	mes
your (familiar sing.)	ton	ta	tes
his/her	son	sa	ses
our	notre	notre	nos
your (polite/pl.)	votre	votre	vos
their	leur	leur	leurs

e.g. **la clé**
(key)

le passeport
(passport)

les billets
(tickets)

sa clé
(his/her key)

son passeport
(his/her passport)

ses billets
(his/her tickets)

Pronouns

· ·

subject		object	
I	je, j'	me	me, m'
you (familiar sing.)	tu	you	te, t'
you (polite/pl.)	vous	you	vous
he/it	il	him/it	le, l'
she/it	elle	her/it	la, l'
we	nous	us	nous
they (masc.)	ils	them	les
they (fem.)	elles	them	les

In French there are two words for *you* – **tu** and **vous**.
Tu is the familiar form, which is used with people
you know well (friends and family), children and
animals. **Vous**, as well as being the plural form of
you, is also the polite way of addressing someone.
You should take care to use this form until the other
person invites you to use the more familiar **tu**.

Object pronouns are placed before the verb, e.g.

il <u>vous</u> aime	(he loves <u>you</u>)
nous <u>la</u> connaissons	(we know <u>her</u>)

However, in commands or requests, object pronouns follow the verb, e.g.

écoutez-<u>le</u> (listen to <u>him</u>)
aidez-<u>moi</u> (help <u>me</u>)

This does not apply to negative commands or requests, e.g.

ne <u>le</u> faites pas (don't do <u>it</u>)

Verbs

• •

There are three main patterns of endings for verbs in French – those ending -**er**, -**ir** and -**re** in the dictionary.

donn**er**	**to give**
je donne	I give
tu donnes	you give
il/elle donne	he/she gives
nous donnons	we give
vous donnez	you give
ils/elles donnent	they give

fin<u>ir</u>	**to finish**
je finis	I finish
tu finis	you finish
il/elle finit	he/she finishes
nous finissons	we finish
vous finissez	you finish
ils/elles finissent	they finish

répond<u>re</u>	**to reply**
je réponds	I reply
tu réponds	you reply
il/elle répond	he/she replies
nous répondons	we reply
vous répondez	you reply
ils/elles répondent	they reply

Irregular verbs

. . . .

Among the most important irregular verbs are the following:

être	**to be**
je suis	I am
tu es	you are
il/elle est	he/she is
nous sommes	we are
vous êtes	you are
ils/elles sont	they are

avoir	to have
j'ai	I have
tu as	you have
il/elle a	he/she has
nous avons	we have
vous avez	you have
ils/elles ont	they have

aller	to go
je vais	I go
tu vas	you go
il/elle va	he/she goes
nous allons	we go
vous allez	you go
ils/elles vont	they go

pouvoir	to be able
je peux	I can
tu peux	you can
il/elle peut	he/she can
nous pouvons	we can
vous pouvez	you can
ils/elles peuvent	they can

Grammar

Past tense

• •

To form the simple past tense of most verbs, e.g.
I finished/I have finished, combine the present tense
of the verb **avoir** (to have) with the past participle
of the verb (**donné**, **fini**, **répondu**), e.g.

j'ai donné	I gave/I have given
j'ai fini	I finished/I have finished
j'ai répondu	I replied/I have replied

Not all verbs take **avoir** as their auxiliary verb;
some verbs take **être** (**je suis...**, **il est...**, etc.).
These are intransitive verbs (which have no object),
e.g.

je suis allé	I went
je suis né	I was born

When the auxiliary verb **être** is used, the past
participle (**allé**, **né**, etc.) becomes adjectival and
agrees with the subject of the verb, e.g.

nous sommes allés	we went *(plural)*
je suis née	I was born *(female)*

A

a(n)	un *m*/une *f*	uñ/ewn
able: *to be able to*	pouvoir	poo-vwar
about		
(approximately)	vers; environ	vehr; ahñ-vee-roñ
(concerning)	au sujet de	oh sew-zheh duh
above	au-dessus (de)	oh duh-sew (duh)
abroad	à l'étranger	a lay-trahñ-zhay
to accept	accepter	ak-sep-tay
access	l'accès *m*	ak-seh
accident	l'accident *m*	ak-see-dahñ
accident & **emergency** **department**	les urgences *fpl*	ewr-zhahñs
accommodation	le logement	lozh-mahñ
address	l'adresse *f*	a-dres
what is the *address?*	quelle est l'adresse?	kel ay la-dres?
admission charge	l'entrée *f*	ahñ-tray
adult	l'adulte *m/f*	a-dewlt
aeroplane	l'avion *m*	a-vyoñ
after	après	apreh
afternoon	l'après-midi *m/f*	a-preh mee-dee
in the afternoon	dans l'après-midi	dahñ la-preh mee-dee
this afternoon	cet après-midi	set a-preh mee-dee
again	encore	ahñkor
against	contre	koñtr
age	l'âge *m*	azh
ago: *a week ago*	il y a une semaine	eel ya ewn suh-men
air-conditioning	la climatisation	klee-ma-tee-za-syoñ
airport	l'aéroport *m*	a-ay-ro-por
airport bus	la navette pour l'aéroport	navet poor la-ay-ro-por
alarm	l'alarme *f*	a-larm
alarm clock	le réveil	ray-vay

alcohol-free	sans alcool	sahñ zal-kol
all	tout(e)/tous/ toutes	too(t)/toos/toot
allergic	allergique	a-lehr-zheek
I'm allergic to...	je suis allergique à...	zhuh swee za-lehr-zheek a...
allergy	l'allergie *f*	a-lehr-zhee
all right (agreed)	d'accord	dakor
are you all right?	ça va?	sa va?
almost	presque	presk
already	déjà	day-zha
also	aussi	oh-see
always	toujours	too-zhoor
a.m.	du matin	dew ma-tañ
ambulance	l'ambulance *f*	ahñ-bew-lahñs
America	l'Amérique *f*	a-may-reek
American	américain(e)	a-may-ree-kañ/ken
and	et	ay
another	un(e) autre	uñ/ewn ohtr
antibiotic	l'antibiotique *m*	ahñ-tee-bee-o-teek
antihistamine	l'antihistaminique *m*	ahñ-tee-ee-sta-mee-neek
any	de (du/de la/des)	duh (dew/duh la/day)
anything	quelque chose	kel- kuh shoz
apartment	l'appartement *m*	a-par-tuh-mahñ
apple	la pomme	pom
appointment	le rendez-vous	rahñ-day-voo
approximately	environ	ahñ-vee-roñ
April	avril	av-reel
arm	le bras	bra
to arrange	arranger	a-rahñ-zhay
arrival	l'arrivée *f*	a-ree-vay
to arrive	arriver	a-ree-vay
to ask	demander	duh-mahñ-day
aspirin	l'aspirine *f*	as-pee-reen
asthma	l'asthme *m*	as-muh

I have asthma	je suis asthmatique	zhuh swee zas-ma-teek
at	à	a
at my/your home	chez moi/vous	shay mwa/voo
at 8 o'clock	à huit heures	a weet ur
at night	la nuit	la nwee
August	août	oo(t)
Australia	l'Australie *f*	oh-stra-lee
Australian	australien(ne)	oh-stra-lyañ/lee-en
autumn	l'automne *m*	oh-ton
available	disponible	dees-poh-neebl

B

baby	le bébé	bay-bay
baby milk (formula)	le lait maternisé	leh ma-tehr-nee-zay
baby's bottle	le biberon	bee-broñ
back (of body)	le dos	doh
backpack	le sac à dos	sak a doh
bad (food, weather)	mauvais(e)	moh-veh/vez
bag	le sac	sak
baggage	les bagages *mpl*	ba-gazh
bank (money)	la banque	bahñk
(river)	la rive; le bord	reev; bor
banknote	le billet de banque	bee-yeh duh bahñk
bar	le bar	bar
bath	le bain	bañ
bathroom	la salle de bains	sal duh bañ
battery (for radio, camera, etc.)	la pile	peel
B&B	la chambre d'hôte	shahñbr doht
to be	être	etr
beach	la plage	plazh
beautiful	beau (belle)	boh (bel)
because	parce que	pars kuh
bed	le lit	lee

double bed	le grand lit; le lit de deux personnes	grahñ lee; lee duh duh pehr-son
single bed	le lit d'une personne	lee dewn pehr-son
twin beds	les lits jumeaux *mpl*	lee zhew-moh
bedroom	la chambre (à coucher)	shahñbr (a koo-shay)
beer	la bière	byehr
before	avant	a-vahñ
to begin	commencer	koh-mahñ-say
behind	derrière	deh-ree-yehr
to belong to	appartenir à	a-par-tuh-neer a
below	sous	soo
beside (next to)	à côté de	a koh-tay duh
better (than)	meilleur(e) (que)	meh-yur (kuh)
between	entre	ahñtr
bicycle	le vélo	vay-loh
big	grand(e); gros(se)	grahñ(d); groh(s)
bigger (than)	plus grand(e) (que); plus gros(se) (que)	plew grahñ(d) (kuh); plew groh(s) (kuh)
bill (restaurant)	l'addition *f*	a-dee-syoñ
(hotel)	la note	not
(for work done)	la facture	fak-tewr
bin (dustbin)	la poubelle	poo-bel
bit: *a bit (of)*	un peu (de)	uñ puh (duh)
bite (animal)	la morsure	mor-sewr
(insect)	la piqûre	pee-kewr
black	noir(e)	nwar
blanket	la couverture	koo-vehr-tewr
blind (person)	aveugle	a-vuh-gluh
blocked	bouché(e)	boo-shay
blood	le sang	sahñ
blue	bleu(e)	bluh
to board (plane, train, etc.)	embarquer	ahñ-bar-kay
boarding card	la carte d'embarquement	kart dahñ-bar-kuh-mahñ

boat	le bateau	ba-toh
(rowing)	la barque	bark
book	le livre	leevr
to book (reserve)	réserver	ray-sehr-vay
booking	la réservation	ray-sehr-va-syoñ
booking office	le bureau de location	bew-roh duh lo-ka-syoñ
bookshop	la librairie	lee-breh-ree
to borrow	emprunter	ahñ-pruñ-tay
bottle	la bouteille	boo-tay-yuh
boy	le garçon	gar-soñ
boyfriend	le copain	ko-pañ
bread	le pain	pañ
bread roll	le petit pain	puh-tee pañ
breakdown (car)	la panne	pan
breakfast	le petit-déjeuner	puh-tee day-zhuh-nay
bridge	le pont	poñ
briefcase	la serviette	sehr-vyet
Britain	la Grande-Bretagne	grahñd-bruh-tan-yuh
British	britannique	bree-ta-neek
broken	cassé(e)	ka-say
my leg is broken	je me suis cassé la jambe	zhuh muh swee ka-say la zhahñb
broken down (car, etc.)	en panne	ahñ pan
brother	le frère	frehr
brown	marron	ma-roñ
building	l'immeuble *m*	ee-muh-bluh
burger	le hamburger	añ-bewr-gehr
bus	le bus	bews
(coach)	le car	kar
bus station	la gare routière	gar roo-tyehr
bus stop	l'arrêt de bus *m*	a-reh duh bews
bus ticket	le ticket de bus	tee-keh duh bews
busy	occupé(e)	o-kew-pay
but	mais	meh

163

to buy	acheter	a-shtay
by (via)	par	par
(beside)	à côté de	a koh-tay duh
by bus	en bus	ahñ bews
by car	en voiture	ahñ vwa-tewr
by ship	en bateau	ahñ ba-toh
by train	en train	ahñ trañ

C

cab (taxi)	le taxi	tak-see
café	le café	ka-fay
internet café	le cybercafé	see-behr-ka-fay
cake (large)	le gâteau	ga-toh
(small)	la pâtisserie; le petit gateau	pa-tee-sree; puh-tee ga-toh
call (telephone)	l'appel *m*	a-pel
to call (speak, phone)	appeler	a-puh-lay
camera	l'appareil photo *m*	a-pa-ray foh-toh
camping gas	le butane	bew-tan
campsite	le camping	kahñ-peeng
can (to be able to)	pouvoir	poo-vwar
(to know how to)	savoir	sa-vwar
I can	je peux/sais	zhuh puh/seh
we can	nous pouvons/ savons	noo poo-voñ/sa-voñ
can	la boîte	bwat
Canada	le Canada	ka-na-da
Canadian	canadien(ne)	ka-na-dyañ/dyen
to cancel	annuler	a-new-lay
car	la voiture	vwa-tewr
card	la carte	kart
careful: *to be careful*	faire attention	fehr a-tahñ-syoñ
be careful!	attention!	a-tahñ-syoñ!

car hire	la location de voitures	lo-ka-syoñ duh vwa-tewr
car insurance	l'assurance automobile *f*	a-sew-rahñs oh-toh-mo-beel
car keys	les clés de voiture *fpl*	klay duh vwa-tewr
car park	le parking	par-keeng
carpet (rug)	le tapis	ta-pee
(fitted)	la moquette	mo-ket
carriage (railway)	la voiture	vwa-tewr
case (suitcase)	la valise	va-leez
cash	l'argent liquide *m*	ar-zhahñ lee-keed
cash dispenser (ATM)	le distributeur automatique (de billets)	dee-stree-bew-tur oh-toh-ma-teek (duh bee-yeh)
castle	le château	sha-toh
catch (bus, train)	prendre	prahñdr
cathedral	la cathédrale	ka-tay-dral
Catholic	catholique	ka-toh-leek
cellphone	le (téléphone) portable	(tay-lay-fon) por-tabl
cent (euro)	un centime	uñ sahñ-teem
central	central(e)	sahñ-tral
central heating	le chauffage central	shoh-fazh sahñ-tral
centre	le centre	sahñtr
cereal	les céréales *fpl*	say-ray-al
chair	la chaise	shez
change (coins)	la monnaie	mo-neh
to change	changer	shahñ-zhay
to *change money*	changer de l'argent	shahñ-zhay duh ar-zhahñ
to *change clothes*	se changer	suh shahñ-zhay
to *change trains*	changer de train	shahñ-zhay duh trañ
Channel (English)	la Manche	mahñsh
charge (fee)	le prix	pree

165

English	French	Pronunciation
to charge a phone	recharger un téléphone	ruh-shar-zhay uñ tay-lay-fon
charger	le chargeur	shar-zhur
cheap	bon marché	boñ mar-shay
cheaper	moins cher	mwañ shehr
to check	vérifier	vay-ree-fyay
to check in	enregistrer	ahñ-ruh-zhee-stray
check-in (desk)	l'enregistrement	ahñ-ruh-zhees-truh-mahñ
(at hotel)	la réception	ray-sep-syoñ
cheers!	santé!	sahñ-tay!
chemist's	la pharmacie	far-ma-see
cheque	le chèque	shek
child	l'enfant m	ahñ-fahñ
children	les enfants	ahñ-fahñ
for children	pour enfants	poor ahñ-fahñ
chilli (vegetable)	le piment	pee-mahñ
(dish)	le chili con carne	shee-lee koñ kar-nay
chips	les frites fpl	freet
chocolate	le chocolat	sho-ko-la
drinking chocolate	le chocolat en poudre	sho-ko-la ahñ poodr
hot chocolate	le chocolat chaud	sho-ko-la shoh
chocolates	les chocolats mpl	sho-ko-la
to choose	choisir	shwa-zeer
Christmas	Noël m	noh-el
church	l'église f	ay-gleez
cigarette	la cigarette	see-ga-ret
cigarette lighter	le briquet	bree-keh
cinema	le cinéma	see-nay-ma
city	la ville	veel
city centre	le centre-ville	sahñtr-veel
clean	propre	propr
to clean	nettoyer	neh-twa-yay
clock	l'horloge f	or-lozh
close by	proche	prosh

closed (shop, etc.)	fermé(e)	fehr-may
clothes	les vêtements *mpl*	vet-mahñ
coach (bus)	le car; l'autocar *m*	kar; oh-oh-kar
coast	la côte	koht
coat	le manteau	mahñ-toh
coffee	le café	ka-fay
white coffee	le café au lait	ka-fay oh leh
black coffee	le café noir	ka-fay nwar
cappuccino	le cappuccino	ka-pew-chee-noh
decaffeinated	le café décaféiné;	ka-fay day-ka-fay-
coffee	le déca	ee-nay; day-ka
coin	la pièce de monnaie	pyes duh mo-neh
Coke®	le Coca®	ko-ka
cold	froid(e)	frwa(d)
I'm cold	j'ai froid	zhay frwa
it's cold	il fait froid	eel feh frwa
cold (illness)	le rhume	rewm
I have a cold	j'ai un rhume	zhay uñ rewm
to come	venir	vuh-neer
(to arrive)	arriver	a-ree-vay
to come back	revenir	ruh-vuh-neer
to come in	entrer	ahñ-tray
come in!	entrez!	ahñ tray!
comfortable	confortable	coñ-for-tabl
company (firm)	la compagnie; la	koñ-pa-nyee;
	société	so-syay-tay
to complain	faire une	fehr ewn
	réclamation	ray-kla-ma-syoñ
complaint	la plainte	plañt
compulsory	obligatoire	ob-lee-ga-twar
computer	l'ordinateur *m*	or-dee-na-tur
concert	le concert	koñ-sehr
concession	la réduction	ray-dewk-syoñ
conference	la conférence	koñ-fay-rahñs
to confirm	confirmer	koñ-feer-may
confirmation	la confirmation	koñ-feer-ma-syoñ

consulate	le consulat	koñ-sew-la
contact lenses	les lentilles de contact *fpl*	lahñ-tee duh koñ-takt
convenient: *it's not convenient*	ça ne m'arrange pas	sa nuh ma-rahñzh pa
to cook (be cooking)	cuisiner	kwee-zee-nay
to cook a meal	préparer un repas	pray-pa-ray uñ ruh-pa
cooker	la cuisinière	kwee-zee-nyehr
to copy	copier	ko-pyay
corner	le coin	kwañ
corridor	le couloir	koo-lwar
cosmetics	les produits de beauté *mpl*	pro-dwee duh boh-tay
cost	le coût	koo
to cost	coûter	koo-tay
how much	ça coûte	sa koot
does it cost?	combien?	koñ-byañ
costume (swimming)	le maillot (de bain)	ma-yoh (duh bañ)
cough	la toux	too
cough mixture	le sirop contre la toux	see-roh koñtr la too
counter (shop, etc.)	le comptoir	koñ-twar
country (not town)	la campagne	kahñ-pa-nyuh
(nation)	le pays	pay-ee
couple (two people)	le couple	koop-luh
a couple of...	deux...	duh...
course (syllabus)	le cours	koor
(of meal)	le plat	pla
cover charge (restaurant)	le couvert	koo-vehr
crash (car)	l'accident *m*; la collision	ak-see-dahñ; ko-lee-zyoñ
cream (food, lotion)	la crème	krem
credit (on mobile phone)	les unités *fpl*	ew-nee-tay
credit card	la carte de crédit	kart duh kray-dee

crisps	les chips *fpl*	sheep
to cross	traverser	tra-vehr-say
crossing (by sea)	la traversée	tra-vehr-say
crossroads	le carrefour; le croisement	kar-foor; krwaz-mahñ
cup	la tasse	tas
customer	le/la client(e)	klee-ahñ(t)
customs	la douane	dwan
(duty)	les droits de douane *mpl*	drwa duh dwan
to cut	couper	koo-pay
to cycle	faire du vélo	fehr dew vay-loh

D

dairy produce	les produits laitiers *mpl*	pro-dwee leh-tyay
dangerous	dangereux(-euse)	dahñ-zhuh-ruh(z)
date	la date	dat
date of birth	la date de naissance	dat duh neh-sahñs
daughter	la fille	fee
day	le jour	zhoor
per day	par jour	par zhoor
every day	tous les jours	too lay zhoor
deaf	sourd(e)	soor(d)
dear (expensive; in letter)	cher (chère)	shehr
debit card	la carte de paiement	kart duh pay-mahñ
decaffeinated coffee	le café décaféiné; le déca	ka-fay day-ka-fay-ce-nay; day-ka
December	décembre	day-sahñbr
to declare	déclarer	day-kla-ray
nothing to declare	rien à déclarer	ryañ na day-kla-ray
delayed	retardé(e)	ruh-tar-day
delicatessen	l'épicerie fine *f*	ay-pees-ree feen
delicious	délicieux(-euse)	day-lee-syuh(z)
deodorant	le déodorant	day-oh-doh-rahñ

to depart	partir	par-teer
department store	le grand magasin	grahñ ma-ga-zañ
departure	le départ	day-par
departure lounge	la salle d'embarquement	sal dahñ-bar-kuh-mahñ
desk (furniture)	le bureau	bew-roh
(information)	l'accueil *m*	a-key
dessert	le dessert	deh-sehr
to develop (photos)	faire développer	fehr day-vloh-pay
diabetic	diabétique	dee-a-bay-teek
I'm diabetic	je suis diabétique	zhuh swee dee-a-bay-teek
to dial (a number)	composer	koñ-poh-say
dialling code	l'indicatif *m*	añ-dee-ka-teef
diesel	le diesel; le gasoil	dee-ay-zel; ga-zwal
diet	le régime	ray-zheem
I'm on a diet	je suis au régime	zhuh swee zoh ray-zheem
different	différent(e)	dee-fay-rahñ(t)
difficult	difficile	dee-fee-seel
dining room	la salle à manger	sal a mahñ-zhay
dinner (evening meal)	le dîner	dee-nay
to have dinner	dîner	dee-nay
direct (train, etc.)	direct(e)	dee-rekt
directions	les indications *fpl*	añ-dee-ka-syoñ
to ask for directions	demander le chemin	duh-mahñ-day luh shuh-mañ
dirty	sale	sal
disabled (person)	handicapé(e)	ahñ-dee-ka-pay
discount	le rabais	ra-beh
to disturb	déranger	day-rahñ-zhay
to dive	plonger	ploñ-zhay
divorced	divorcé(e)	dee-vor-say
dizzy	pris(e) de vertige	pree(z) duh vehr-teezh
to do	faire	fehr
doctor	le médecin	may-dsañ

documents	les papiers *mpl*	pa-pyay
dollar	le dollar	do-lar
door	la porte	port
double bed	le grand lit	grahñ lee
double room	la chambre pour deux personnes	shahñbr poor duh pehr-son
down: to go down	descendre	deh-sahñdr
downstairs	en bas	ahñ ba
dress	la robe	rob
drink	la boisson	bwa-soñ
to drink	boire	bwar
drinking water	l'eau potable *f*	oh po-tabl
to drive	conduire	koñ-dweer
driver (of car)	le conducteur; la conductrice	koñ-dewk-tur; koñ-dewk-trees
driving licence	le permis de conduire	pehr-mee duh koñ-dweer
dry	sec (sèche)	sek/sesh
to dry	sécher	say-shay
dry-cleaner's	le pressing	preh-seeng
during	pendant	pahñ-dahñ
duty-free	hors taxe	or tax

E

each	chacun/chacune	sha-kuñ/sha-kewn
earlier	plus tôt	plew-toh
early	tôt	toh
east	l'est *m*	est
Easter	Pâques	pak
easy	facile	fa-seel
to eat	manger	mahñ-zhay
either ... or	soit ... soit	swa ... swa
Elastoplast®	le sparadrap	spa-ra-dra
electric	électrique	ay-lek-treek
electricity	l'électricité *f*	ay-lek-tree-see-tay

electronic	électronique	ay-lek-tro-neek
elevator	l'ascenseur *m*	a-sahñ-sur
e-mail	l'e-mail *m*	ee-mehl
to e-mail	envoyer un e-mail	ahñ-vwa-yay uñ nee-mehl
e-mail address (on forms)	l'adresse électronique; le mél	a-dres ay-lek-tro-neek; mayl
embassy	l'ambassade *f*	ahñ-ba-sad
emergency	l'urgence *f*	ewr-zhahñs
emergency exit	la sortie de secours	sor-tee duh skoor
end	la fin	fañ
engaged (to be married)	fiancé(e)	fee-ahñ-say
(phone, toilet, etc.)	occupé(e)	o-kew-pay
engine	le moteur	moh-tur
England	l'Angleterre *f*	ahñ-gluh-tehr
English	anglais(e)	ahñ-gleh(z)
(language)	l'anglais *m*	ahñ-gleh
to enjoy	aimer	ay-may
I enjoyed the trip	le voyage m'a plu	vwa-yazh ma plew
enough	assez	a-say
that's enough	ça suffit	sa sew-fee
enquiry desk	les renseignements *mpl*	rahñ-seh-nyuh-mahñ
to enter	entrer	ahñ-tray
entrance	l'entrée *f*	ahñ-tray
entrance fee	le prix d'entrée	pree dahñ-tray
equal	égal	ay-gal
error	l'erreur *f*	eh-rur
essential	indispensable	añ-dee-spahñ-sabl
euro (unit of currency)	l'euro *m*	uh-roh
Europe	l'Europe *f*	ur-op
European	européen(ne)	ur-o-pay-añ/en
evening	le soir	swar
this evening	ce soir	suh swar
in the evening	le soir	swar

every	chaque	shak
everyone	tout le monde	too luh moñd
everything	tout	too
everywhere	partout	par-too
example: *for example*	par exemple	par eg-zahñpl
excellent	excellent(e)	ek-seh-lahñ(t)
exchange	l'échange *m*	ay-shahñzh
exchange rate	le taux de change	toh duh shahñzh
to exchange	échanger	ay-shahñ-zhay
to excuse: *excuse me!*	excusez-moi!	ek-skew-zay-mwa!
(to get by)	pardon!	par-doñ!
exhibition	l'exposition *f*	ek-spoh-zee-syoñ
exit	la sortie	sor-tee
expensive	cher (chère)	shehr
to expire (ticket, passport, etc.)	expirer	ek-spee-ray
to explain	expliquer	ek-splee-kay
extra (additional)	supplémentaire	sew-play-mahñ-tehr
(more)	de plus	duh plews
eye	l'œil *m*	uhy
eyes	les yeux	yıh

F

face	le visage	vee-zazh
facilities	les équipements *mpl*	ay-keep-mahñ
to fall	tomber	toñ-bay
he has fallen	il est tombé	eel eh toñ-bay
family	la famille	fa-mee
far	loin	lwañ
is it far?	c'est loin?	say lwañ?
fare (bus, etc.)	le prix du billet	pree dew bee-yeh
farm	la ferme	fehrm
fast	rapide	ra-peed

too fast	trop vite	troh veet
father	le père	pehr
fault (defect)	le défaut	day-foh
it's not my fault	ce n'est pas de ma faute	suh nay pa duh ma foht
fax	le fax	fax
February	février	fay-vryay
to feel	sentir	sahñ-teer
I feel sick	j'ai la nausée	zhay la noh-say
I don't feel well	je ne me sens pas bien	zhuh nuh muh sahñ pa byañ
feet	les pieds *mpl*	pyay
fever	la fièvre	fyevr
few	peu de	puh duh
a few	quelques-un(e)s	kel-kuh-zuñ/zewn
fiancé(e)	le fiancé; la fiancée	fee-yahñ-say
to fill in (form)	remplir	rahñ-pleer
film (movie)	le film	feelm
(for camera)	la pellicule	peh-lee-kewl
to find	trouver	troo-vay
fine (penalty)	la contravention	koñ-tra-vahñ-syoñ
finger	le doigt	dwa
to finish	finir	fee-neer
finished	fini(e)	fee-nee
fire	le feu; l'incendie *m*	fuh; añ-sahñ-dee
fire alarm	l'alarme d'incendie *f*	a-larm dañ-sahñ-dee
fire escape (staircase)	l'échelle de secours *f*	ay-shel duh skoor
first	premier(-ière)	pruh-myay/myehr
first aid	les premiers secours *mpl*	pruh-myay skoor
first-class	de première classe	duh pruh-myehr klas
first name	le prénom	pray-noñ
fish	le poisson	pwa-soñ
fishing	la pêche	pesh
to go fishing	aller à la pêche	a-lay a la pesh

fit (medical)	l'attaque *f*	a-tak
to fit: it doesn't fit me	ça ne me va pas	sa nuh muh va pa
to fix (repair)	réparer	ray-pa-ray
can you fix it?	vous pouvez le réparer?	voo poo-vay luh ray-pa-ray?
flash (for camera)	le flash	flash
flat (apartment)	l'appartement *m*	a-par-tuh-mahñ
flavour	le goût	goo
(of ice cream, etc.)	le parfum	par-fuñ
flight	le vol	vol
floor (of room)	le sol	sol
(storey)	l'étage	ay-tazh
(on the) ground floor	(au) rez-de-chaussée	(oh) ray-duh-shoh-say
(on the) first floor	(au) premier étage	(oh) pruh-myayr ay-tazh
flour	la farine	fa-reen
flower	la fleur	flur
flu	la grippe	greep
to fly (person)	aller en avion	a-lay ahñ na-vyoñ
(bird)	voler	vo-lay
food	la nourriture	noo-ree-tewr
food poisoning	l'intoxication alimentaire *f*	añ-tok-see-ka-syoñ a-lee-mahñ-tehr
foot	le pied	pyay
to go on foot	aller à pied	a-lay a pyay
for	pour	poor
for me/you/us	pour moi/vous/nous	poor mwa/voo/noo
for him/her/them	pour lui/elle/eux	poor lwee/el/uh
forbidden	interdit(e)	añ-tehr-dee(t)
foreign	étranger(-ère)	ay-trahñ-zhay/zhehr
fork (for eating)	la fourchette	foor-shet
form (document)	le formulaire	for-mew-lehr
(shape, style)	la forme	form

fortnight	la quinzaine	kañ-zen
fountain	la fontaine	foñ-ten
fragile	fragile	fra-zheel
France	la France	frahñs
in/to France	en France	ahñ frahñs
free (not occupied)	libre	leebr
(costing nothing)	gratuit(e)	gra-twee(t)
freezer	le congélateur	koñ-zhayla-tur
French	français(e)	frahñ-seh(z)
(language)	le français	frahñ-seh
French fries	les frites *fpl*	freet
fresh	frais (fraîche)	freh/fresh
Friday	vendredi	vahñ-druh-dee
fried	frit(e)	free(t)
friend	l'ami(e) *m/f*	a-mee
from	de	duh
I'm from England	je suis anglais(e)	zhuh swee zahñ-gleh(z)
I'm from Scotland	je suis écossais(e)	zhuh swee zay-ko-seh(z)
front	le devant	duh-vahñ
in front of...	devant...	duh-vahñ...
frozen	gelé(e)	zhuh-lay
fruit	le fruit	frwee
fruit juice	le jus de fruit	jew duh frwee
full (container)	plein(e)	plañ/plen
(e.g. hall)	complet(-ète)	koñ-pleh(t)
full board	la pension complète	pahñ-syoñ koñ-plet
furnished	meublé(e)	muh-blay

G

gallery (art)	le musée (d'art)	mew-zay (dar)
game	le jeu	zhuh
garage (for petrol)	la station-service	sta-syoñ-sehr-vees
(for parking, repair)	le garage	ga-razh

garden	le jardin	zhar-dañ
garlic	l'ail *m*	a-yuh
gate	la porte	port
gents' (toilet)	les toilettes pour hommes *fpl*	twa-let poor om
German (language)	allemand(e)	al-mahñ(d)
	l'allemand *m*	al-mahñ
Germany	l'Allemagne *f*	a-luh-ma-nyuh
to get (obtain)	obtenir	ob-tuh-neer
(to fetch)	aller chercher	a-lay shehr-shay
to get in (vehicle)	monter	moñ-tay
to get off (bus, etc.)	descendre	deh-sahñdr
gift	le cadeau	ka-doh
gift shop	la boutique de souvenirs	boo-teek duh soo-vneer
girl	la fille	fee
girlfriend	la copine	ko-peen
to give	donner	do-nay
to give back	rendre	rahñdr
glass	le verre	vehr
a glass of water	un verre d'eau	uñ vehr doh
glasses (spectacles)	les lunettes *fpl*	lew-net
gluten	le gluten	glew-ten
to go	aller	a-lay
I'm going to... (I will go to)	je vais à...	zhuh veh a...
I'm going to... (I intend to)	je vais...	zhuh veh...
we're going to hire a car	nous allons louer une voiture	noo za-loñ loo-ay ewn vwa-tewr
to go back	retourner	ruh-toor-nay
to go in	entrer	ahñ-tray
to go out (leave)	sortir	sor-teer
good	bon (bonne)	boñ (bon)
(that's) good!	(c'est) bien!	(say) byañ!
good afternoon	bonjour	boñ-zhoor

H

goodbye	au revoir	oh ruh-vwar
goodnight	bonne nuit	bon nwee
grandchildren	les petits-enfants	puh-tee zahñ-fahñ
grandparents	les grands-parents	grahñ-pa-rahñ
grape	le raisin	reh-zañ
great (big)	grand(e)	grahñ(d)
(wonderful)	génial	zhay-nyal
Great Britain	la Grande-Bretagne	grahñd-bruh-ta-nyuh
green	vert(e)	vehr(t)
greengrocer's	le magasin de fruits et légumes	ma-ga-zañ duh frwee zay lay-gewm
grilled	grillé(e)	gree-yay
grocer's	l'épicerie *f*	ay-pee-sree
ground floor	le rez-de-chaussée	ray-duh-shoh-say
on the ground floor	au rez-de-chaussée	oh ray-duh-shoh-say
group	le groupe	groop
guest (in house)	l'invité(e)	añ-vee-tay
(in hotel)	le/la client(e)	klee-ahñ(t)
guesthouse	la pension	pahñ-syoñ
guide (tourist)	le/la guide	geed
guidebook	le guide	geed
guided tour	la visite guidée	vee-zeet gee-day

H

hair	les cheveux *mpl*	shuh-vuh
hairdryer	le sèche-cheveux	sesh-shuh-vuh
half	la moitié	mwa-tyay
half an hour	une demi-heure	ewn duh-mee-ur
half board	la demi-pension	duh-mee-pahñ-syoñ
ham (cooked)	le jambon	zhahñ-boñ
(cured)	le jambon cru	zhahñ-boñ krew
hamburger	le hamburger	ahñ-bur-ger
hand	la main	mañ
handbag	le sac à main	sak a mañ

handicapped	handicapé(e)	ahñ-dee-ka-pay
to happen	arriver; se passer	suh pa-say
what happened?	qu'est-ce qui s'est passé?	kes kee say pa-say?
happy	heureux(-euse)	uh-ruh(z)
hard (not soft)	dur(e)	dewr
(not easy)	difficile	dee-fee-seel
to have	avoir	av-war
to have to	devoir	duh-vwar
hay fever	le rhume des foins	rewm day fwañ
he	il	eel
head	la tête	tet
headache	le mal de tête	mal duh tet
I have a headache	j'ai mal à la tête	zhay mal a la tet
health	la santé	sahñ-tay
to hear	entendre	ahñ-tahñdr
heart	le cœur	kur
heartburn	les brûlures d'estomac *fpl*	brew-lewr d'es-toh-ma
heating	le chauffage	shoh-fazh
heavy	lourd(e)	loor(d)
hello	bonjour	boñ-zhoor
(on telephone)	allô?	a-loh?
help!	au secours!	oh skoor!
can you help me?	vous pouvez m'aider?	voo poo-vay meh-day?
her	son/sa/ses	soñ/sa/say
her passport	son passeport	soñ pas-por
her suitcases	ses valises	say va-leez
herbal tea	la tisane; l'infusion *f*	tee-zan; añ-few-zyoñ
here	ici	ee-see
here is...	voici...	vwa-see...
hi!	salut!	sa-lew!
high	haut(e)	oh(t)
him	lui	lwee
to hire	louer	loo-ay

hired car	la voiture de location	la vwa-tewr duh lo-ka-syoñ
his	son/sa/ses	soñ/sa/say
his passport	son passeport	soñ pas-por
his suitcases	ses valises	say va-leez
holiday	les vacances *mpl*	va-kahñs
on holiday	en vacances	ahñ va-kahñs
home	la maison	meh-zoñ
at my/your/our home	chez moi/vous/ nous	shay mwa/voo/noo
honey	le miel	myel
I hope so/not	j'espère que oui/ non	zheh-spehr kuh wee/ noñ
hospital	l'hôpital *m*	o-pee-tal
hostel (youth hostel)	l'auberge de jeunesse *f*	oh-behrzh duh zhuh-nes
hot	chaud(e)	shoh(d)
I'm hot	j'ai chaud	zhay shoh
it's hot (weather)	il fait chaud	eel feh shoh
hotel	l'hôtel *m*	oh-tel
hour	l'heure *f*	ur
half an hour	une demi-heure	ewn duh-mee ur
house	la maison	meh-soñ
house wine	le vin en pichet	vañ ahñ pee-sheh
how	comment	ko-mahñ
how much/many?	combien?	koñ-byañ?
how are you?	comment allez-vous?	ko-mahñ ta-lay voo?
hungry: *to be hungry*	avoir faim	avwar fañ
I'm hungry	j'ai faim	zhay fañ
hurry: *I'm in a hurry*	je suis pressé(e)	zhuh swee preh-say
to hurt: *to hurt somebody*	faire du mal à quelqu'un	fehr dew mal a kel-kuñ
that hurts	ça fait mal	sa feh mal
husband	le mari	ma-ree

I

I	je	zhuh
ice	la glace	glas
(cube)	le glaçon	gla-soñ
with/without ice	avec/sans glaçons	a-vek/sañ gla-soñ
ice cream	la glace	glas
identity card	la carte d'identité	kart dee-dahñ-tee-tay
if	si	see
ill	malade	ma-lad
illness	la maladie	ma-la-dee
important	important(e)	añ-por-tahñ(t)
impossible	impossible	añ-po-seebl
in	dans	dahñ
in two hours' time	dans deux heures	dahñ duh zur
in front of	devant	duh-vahñ
included	compris(e)	koñ-pree(z)
indigestion	l'indigestion *f*	añ-dee-zhes-tyoñ
information	les renseignements *mpl*	rahñ-seh-nyuh-mahñ
injured	blessé(e)	bleh-say
inside	à l'intérieur	a lañ-tay-ryur
instead of	au lieu de	oh lyuh duh
insurance	l'assurance *f*	a-sew-rahñs
insurance certificate	l'attestation d'assurance *f*	a-tes-ta-syoñ da-sew-rahñs
insured	assuré(e)	a-sew-ray
interesting	intéressant(e)	añ-tay-reh-sahñ(t)
international	international(e)	añ-tehr-na-syo-nal
into	dans; en	dahñ; ahñ
into town	en ville	ahñ veel
Ireland	l'Irlande *f*	eer-lahñd
Irish	irlandais(e)	eer-lahñ-deh(z)
iron (for clothes)	le fer à repasser	fehr a ruh-pa-say
is	est	ay
island	l'île *f*	eel

it	il/elle	eel/el
Italian	italien(ne)	ee-ta-lyañ/lyen
Italy	l'Italie *f*	ee-ta-lee
to itch	démanger	day-mañ-zhay
it itches	ça me démange	sa muh day-mahñzh

J

January	janvier	jahñ-vyay
jeweller's	la bijouterie	bee-zhoo-tree
jewellery	les bijoux *mpl*	bee-zhoo
job	le travail; l'emploi *m*	tra-va-yuh; ahñ-plwa
journey	le voyage	vwa-yazh
juice	le jus	jew
fruit juice	le jus de fruit	jew duh fwree
orange juice	le jus d'orange	jew do-rahñzh
July	juillet	zhwee-yeh
June	juin	zhwañ

K

to keep (retain)	garder	gar-day
keep the change	gardez la monnaie	gar-day la mo-neh
key	la clé/clef	klay
car key	la clé/clef de la voiture	klay duh vwa-tewr
kilo(gram)	le kilo	kee-loh
kilometre	le kilomètre	kee-loh-metr
kiosk (newsstand)	le kiosque	kee-yosk
kitchen	la cuisine	kwee-zeen
knee	le genou	zhuh-noo
knife	le couteau	koo-toh
to know (how to do, to be aware of)	savoir	sa-vwar
(person, place)	connaître	ko-nehtr
I don't know	je ne sais pas	zhuh nuh seh pa
I don't know Paris	je ne connais pas Paris	zhuh nuh ko-neh pa pa-ree

L

ladies' (toilet)	les toilettes pour dames *fpl*	twa-let poor dam
lamb	l'agneau *m*	a-nyoh
to land	atterrir	a-teh-reer
language	la langue	lahñg
large	grand(e)	grahñ(d)
last	dernier(-ière)	dehr-nyay/nyehr
last month	le mois dernier	mwa dehr-nyay
last night (evening)	hier soir	ee-yehr swar
(night-time)	la nuit dernière	nwee dehr-nyehr
last week	la semaine dernière	suh-men dehr-nyehr
late	tard	tar
later	plus tard	plew tar
lavatory	les toilettes *fpl*	twa-let
to leave (depart for)	partir	par-teer
(depart from)	quitter	kee-tay
(to leave behind)	laisser	leh-say
to leave for Paris	partir pour Paris	par-teer poor pa-ree
to leave London	quitter Londres	kee-tay loñdr
left: *on/to the left*	à gauche	a gohsh
left-luggage (office)	la consigne	koñ-see-nyuh
leg	la jambe	zhahñb
lemon	le citron	see-troñ
lemonade	la limonade	lee-mo-nad
lens (contact lens)	la lentille	lahñ-tee
less	moins	mo-añ
less than	moins de	mwañ duh
letter	la lettre	letr
lift (elevator)	l'ascenseur *m*	a-sahñ-sur
light (not heavy)	léger(-ère)	lay-zhay/zhehr
light	la lumière	lewm-yehr
have you got a light?	avez-vous du feu?	a-vay-voo dew fuh?
like (preposition)	comme	kom

183

English - French

like this	comme ça	kom sa
to like	aimer	eh-may
I like coffee	j'aime le café	zhem luh ka-fay
I don't like coffee	je n'aime pas le café	zhuh nem pa luh ka-fay
I'd like...	je voudrais...	zhuh voo-dreh...
we'd like...	nous voudrions...	noo voo-dryoñ...
line (queue)	la file	feel
(telephone)	la ligne	lee-nyuh
to listen to	écouter	ay-koo-tay
litre	le litre	leetr
little	petit(e)	puh-tee(t)
a little...	un peu de...	uñ puh duh...
to live (in a place)	vivre; habiter	veevr; a-bee-tay
I live in London	j'habite à Londres	zha-beet a lahñdr
to lock	fermer à clé/clef	fer-may a klay
London	Londres	loñdr
to/in London	à Londres	a loñdr
long	long(ue)	loñ(g)
for a long time	longtemps	loñ-tahñ
to look after	garder	gar-day
to look at	regarder	ruh-gar-day
to look for	chercher	shehr-shay
to lose	perdre	pehrdr
lost (object)	perdu(e)	pehr-dew
I've lost...	j'ai perdu...	zhay pehr-dew...
I'm lost	je suis perdu(e)	zhuh swee pehr-dew
lost property office	le bureau des objets trouvés	bew-roh day zob-zheh troo-vay
lot: *a lot of*	beaucoup de	boh-koo duh
loud	fort(e)	for(t)
lounge (in hotel, airport)	le salon	sa-loñ
love	l'amour *m*	a-moor
to love (person)	aimer	eh-may
I love you	je t'aime	zhuh tem
(food, activity, etc.)	adorer	a-do-ray

I love swimming	j'adore nager	zha-dor na-zhay
lovely	beau (belle)	boh (bel)
low	bas (basse)	ba(s)
luck	la chance	shahñs
lucky	chanceux(-euse)	shahñ-suh(z)
luggage	les bagages *mpl*	ba-gazh
luggage trolley	le chariot	sha-ryoh
lunch	le déjeuner	day-zhuh-nay
luxury	le luxe	lewx

M

machine	la machine	ma-sheen
magazine	la revue; le magazine	ruh-vew; ma-ga-zeen
mail	le courrier	koo-ryay
by mail	par la poste	par la post
main	principal(e)	prañ-see-pal
to make	faire	fehr
make-up	le maquillage	ma-kee-yazh
male (person)	masculin	mas-kew-lañ
man	l'homme *m*	om
manager	le/la directeur(-trice)	dee-rek-tur/ dee-rek-trees
many	beaucoup de	boh-koo duh
map	la carte	kart
road map	la carte routière	kart roo-tyehr
street map	le plan de la ville	plahñ duh la veel
March	mars	mars
market	le marché	mar-shay
married	marié(e)	ma-ryay
I'm married	je suis marié(e)	zhuh swee ma-ryay
Mass (in church)	la messe	mes
match (sport)	le match	match
matches	les allumettes *fpl*	alew-met
to matter: it doesn't matter	ça ne fait rien	sa nuh feh ryañ

English	French	Pronunciation
what's the matter?	qu'est-ce qu'il y a?	kes keel ya?
May	mai	meh
me	moi	mwa
meal	le repas	ruh-pa
to mean	vouloir dire	voo-lwar deer
what does this mean?	qu'est-ce que ça veut dire?	kes kuh sa vuh deer?
meat	la viande	vyahñd
medicine	le médicament	may-dee-ka-mahñ
Mediterranean Sea	la Méditerranée	may-dee-tay-ra-nay
to meet	rencontrer	rahñ-koñ-tray
meeting	la réunion	ray-ew-nyoñ
men	les hommes *mpl*	om
to mend	réparer	ray-pa-ray
menu (set meal)	le menu	muh-new
(card)	la carte	kart
message	le message	meh-sazh
meter	le compteur	koñ-tur
metre	le mètre	metr
metro	le métro	may-troh
metro station	la station de métro	sta-syoñ duh may-troh
midday	midi	mee-dee
at midday	à midi	a mee-dee
middle	le milieu	mee-lyuh
midnight	minuit	mee-nwee
at midnight	à minuit	a mee-nwee
mild (weather, cheese)	doux (douce)	doo(s)
(curry)	peu épicé(e)	puh ay-pee-say
(tobacco)	léger(-ère)	lay-zhay/zhehr
milk	le lait	leh
baby milk (formula)	le lait maternisé	leh ma-tehr-nee-zay
fresh milk	le lait frais	leh freh
soya milk	le lait de soja	leh duh so-zha
with/without milk	avec/sans lait	a-vek/sahñ leh
to mind: *do you mind if I...?*	ça vous gêne si je...?	sa voo zhen see zhuh...?

I don't mind	ça m'est égal	sa may tay-gal
do you mind?	vous permettez?	voo pehr-meh-tay?
mineral water	l'eau minérale *f*	oh mee-nay-ral
minute	la minute	mee-newt
to miss (train, flight, etc.)	rater	ra-tay
Miss	Mademoiselle	ma-dmwa-zel
missing (disappeared)	disparu(e)	dee-spa-rew
mistake	l'erreur *f*	eh-rur
mobile (phone)	le portable	por-tabl
mobile number	le numéro de portable	new-may-roh duh por-tabl
moment: *at the moment*	en ce moment	ahñ suh mo-mahñ
Monday	lundi	luñ-dee
money	l'argent *m*	ar-zhahñ
I have no money	je n'ai pas d'argent	zhuh nay pa dar-zhahñ
month	le mois	mwa
this month	ce mois-ci	suh mwa-see
next month	le mois prochain	luh mwa pro-shañ
more	encore	ahñ-kor
more wine	plus de vin	plews duh vañ
more than	plus de	plews duh
morning	le matin	ma-tañ
in the morning	le matin	luh ma-tañ
tomorrow morning	demain matin	duh-mañ ma-tañ
mother	la mère	mehr
motorbike	la moto	moh-toh
motorway	l'autoroute *f*	oh-toh-root
mountain	la montagne	moñ-ta-nyuh
mouth	la bouche	boosh
to move	bouger	boo-zhay
movie	le film	feelm
Mr	Monsieur	muh-syuh
Mrs	Madame	ma-dam
Ms	Madame	ma-dam

much: *too much*	trop	troh
museum	le musée	mew-zay
music	la musique	mew-zeek
must	devoir	duh-vwar
my	mon/ma/mes	moñ/ma/may

N

name	le nom	luh noñ
my name is...	je m'appelle...	zhuh ma-pel...
what is your name?	comment vous appelez-vous?	ko-mahñ voo za-play voo?
nationality	la nationalité	na-syo-na-lee-tay
near	près de	preh duh
is it near?	c'est près d'ici?	say preh dee-see?
to need (to)	avoir besoin de	a-vwar buh-zwañ duh
I need...	j'ai besoin...	zhay buh-zwañ...
new	nouveau(-elle)	noo-voh/vel
news (TV, etc.)	les informations *fpl*	añ-for-ma-syoñ
newspaper	le journal	zhoor-nal
New Zealand	la Nouvelle-Zélande	noo-vel zay-lahñd
next	prochain(e)	pro-shañ/shen
(after)	ensuite	ahñ-sweet
next Monday	lundi prochain	luñ-dee pro-shañ
the next train	le prochain train	luh pro-shañ trañ
next week	la semaine prochaine	la suh-men pro-shen
next to	à côté de	a ko-tay duh
nice	beau (belle)	boh (bel)
(enjoyable)	bon (bonne)	boñ (bon)
(person)	sympathique	sañ-pa-teek
night (night-time)	la nuit	nwee
(evening)	le soir	swar
last night	hier soir	ee-yeehr swar
tomorrow night (evening)	demain soir	duh-mañ swar
tonight	ce soir	suh swar

nightclub	la boîte de nuit	bwat duh nwee
no	non	noñ
(without)	sans	sahñ
no thanks	non merci	noñ mehr-see
noisy: *it's very*	il y a beaucoup	eel ya boh-koo
noisy	de bruit	duh brwee
non-smoking (seat,	non-fumeurs	noñ few-mur
compartment)		
north	le nord	nor
Northern Ireland	l'Irlande du Nord *f*	eer-lahñd dew nor
nose	le nez	nay
not	ne ... pas	nuh ... pa
I am not...	je ne suis pas...	zhuh nuh swee pa...
note (banknote)	le billet	bee-yeh
nothing	rien	ryañ
November	novembre	no-vahñbr
now	maintenant	mañ-tuh-nahñ
number (quantity)	le nombre	noñbr
(of room, house)	le numéro	new-may-roh
phone number	le numéro de	new-may-roh duh
	téléphone	tay-lay-fon

O

October	octobre	ok-tobr
of	de	duh
a glass of...	un verre de...	uñ vehr duh...
made of...	en...	ahñ...
office	le bureau	bew-roh
often	souvent	soo-vahñ
oil (for car, food)	l'huile *f*	weel
OK (agreed)	d'accord	da-kor
(good)	bon (bonne)	boñ (bon)
old	vieux (vieille)	vyuh (vyeh-yuh)
how old are you?	quel âge avez-vous?	kel azh a-vay voo?
I'm ... years old	j'ai ... ans	zhay ... ahñ

189

on (light)	allumé(e)	a-lew-may
(machine, etc.)	en marche	ahñ marsh
on the table	sur la table	sewr la tabl
on time	à l'heure	a lur
once	une fois	ewn fwa
onion	l'oignon *m*	oh-nyoñ
open	ouvert(e)	oo-vehr(t)
opposite	en face de	ahñ fas duh
or	ou	oo
orange (fruit)	l'orange	o-rahñzh
(colour)	orange	o-rahñzh
orange juice	le jus d'orange	jew do-rahñzh
order: *out of order*	en panne	ahñ pan
to order	commander	ko-mahñ-day
organic	bio	bee-yo
other	autre	ohtr
have you any others?	vous en avez d'autres?	voo zahñ na-vay dohtr?
our (singular)	notre	notr
(plural)	nos	noh
our room	notre chambre	notr shahñbr
our baggage	nos bagages	noh ba-gazh
outside	dehors	duh·or

P

to pack (luggage)	faire ses bagages	fehr say ba-gazh
package	le paquet	pa-kay
page	la page	pazh
paid	payé(e)	pay-yay
I've paid	j'ai payé	zhay pay-yay
pain	la douleur	doo-lur
painful	douloureux(-euse)	doo-loo-ruh(z)
painkiller	l'analgésique *m*	a-nal-zhay-zeek
pants (underwear)	le slip, la culotte	sleep, kew-lot
(trousers)	le pantalon	pahñ-ta-loñ

paper	le papier	pa-pyay
pardon?	comment?	ko-mahñ?
parents	les parents	pa-rahñ
park	le parc	park
to park	garer (la voiture)	ga-ray (la vwa-tewr)
party (group)	le groupe	groop
(celebration)	la fête; la soirée	fet; swa-ray
pass (bus, train)	la carte	kart
passenger	le passager; la passagère	pa-sa-zhay; pa-sa-zhehr
passport	le passeport	pas-por
pasta	les pâtes fpl	pat
pastry	la pâte	pat
(cake)	la pâtisserie	pa-tee-sree
to pay	payer	pay-yay
I'd like to pay	je voudrais payer	zhuh voo-dreh pay-yay
where do I pay?	où est-ce qu'il faut payer?	oo es keel foh pay-yay?
peanut	la cacahuète	ka-ka-wet
peanut allergy	l'allergie aux cacahuètes f	a-lehr-zhee oh ka-ka-wet
peas	les petits pois mpl	puh-tee pwa
pen	le stylo	stee-loh
pensioner	le/la retraité(e)	ruh-treh-tay
people	les gens mpl	zhahñ
pepper (spice)	le poivre	pwavr
(vegetable)	le poivron	pwa-vroñ
per: per day	par jour	par zhoor
per hour	à l'heure	a lur
per person	par personne	par pehr-son
per week	par semaine	par suh-men
performance	le spectacle	spek-takl
person	la personne	pehr-son
petrol	l'essence f	eh-sahñs
unleaded petrol	l'essence sans plomb f	eh-sahñs sahñ ploñ

petrol station	la station-service	sta-syoñ ser-vees
pharmacy	la pharmacie	far-ma-see
to photocopy	photocopier	foh-toh-ko-pyay
photograph	la photo	foh-toh
to take a photograph	prendre une photo	prahñdr ewn foh-toh
piece	le morceau	mor-soh
pink	rose	roz
place of birth	le lieu de naissance	lyuh duh neh-sahñs
plan (map)	le plan	plahñ
plate	l'assiette *f*	a-syet
platform (railway)	le quai	keh
which platform?	quel quai?	kel keh?
play (at theatre)	la pièce	pyes
please	s'il vous plaît	seel voo pleh
pleased to meet you	enchanté(e)	ahñ-shahñ-tay
poisonous	vénéneux(-euse)	vay-nay-nuh(z)
police (force)	la police	po-lees
police station	le commissariat	ko-mee-sa-rya
(in a rural area)	la gendarmerie	zhahñ-dar-mree
pork	le porc	por
port (seaport)	le port	por
porter (for luggage)	le porteur	por-tur
possible	possible	po-seebl
post (letters)	le courrier	koo-ryay
by post	par courrier	par koo-ryay
to post	poster	po-stay
postbox	la boîte aux lettres	bwat oh letr
postcard	la carte postale	kart po-stal
post office	la poste	post
potato	la pomme de terre	pom duh tehr
pound (weight, money)	la livre	leevr
to prefer	préférer	pray-fa-yray
pregnant	enceinte	ahñ-sañt

present (gift)	le cadeau	ka-doh
pretty	joli(e)	zho-lee
price	le prix	pree
price list	le tarif	ta-reef
problem	le problème	pro-blem
prohibited	interdit(e)	añ-tehr-dee(t)
public	public(-ique)	pew-bleek
pudding	le dessert	deh-sehr
to pull	tirer	tee-ray
purse	le porte-monnaie	port-mo-neh
to push	pousser	poo-say

Q

quarter	le quart	kar
question	la question	ke-styoñ
quick	rapide	ra-peed
quickly	vite	veet
quiet (place)	tranquille	trahñ-keel
quite (rather)	assez	a-say
(completely)	complètement	koñ-plet-mahñ
quite good	pas mal	pa mal

R

railway	le chemin de fer	shuh-mañ duh fehr
railway station	la gare	gar
to rain: *it's raining*	il pleut	eel pluh
rare (steak)	saignant(e)	say-nyahñ(t)
rate of exchange	le taux de change	toh duh shahñzh
raw	cru(e)	crew
razor	le rasoir	ra-zwar
razor blades	les lames de rasoir *fpl*	lam duh ra-zwar
ready	prêt(e)	preh/pret
receipt	le reçu	ruh-sew
reception (desk)	la réception	ray-sep-syoñ

R

English – French

to recommend	recommander	ruh-ko-mahñ-day
red	rouge	roozh
reduction	la réduction	ray-dewk-syoñ
remember	se souvenir de	suh soo-vuh-neer duh
I don't remember	je ne m'en souviens pas	zhuh nuh mahñ soo-vyañ pa
to repair	réparer	ray-pa-ray
to repeat	répéter	ray-pay-tay
to report (theft, etc.)	déclarer	day-kla-ray
reservation	la réservation	ray-zehr-va-syoñ
to reserve	réserver	ray-zehr-vay
reserved	réservé(e)	ray-zehr-vay
rest (relaxation)	le repos	ruh-poh
(remainder)	le reste	rest
restaurant	le restaurant	reh-stoh-rahñ
retired	retraité(e)	ruh-treh-tay
to return (to a place)	retourner	ruh-toor-nay
return ticket	le billet aller-retour	bee-yeh a-lay-ruh-toor
rice	le riz	ree
right (correct)	exact(e)	eg-zakt
right (not left)	la droite	drwat
on/to the right	à droite	a drwat
river	la rivière	ree-vyehr
(flowing to sea)	le fleuve	fluhv
Riviera (French)	la Côte d'Azur	koht da-zewr
road	la route	root
road map	la carte routière	kart roo-tyehr
road sign	le panneau	pa-noh
roll (bread)	le petit pain	puh-tee pañ
room (in house)	la pièce	pyes
(in hotel)	la chambre	shahñbr
double room	la chambre pour deux personnes	shahñbr poor duh pehr-son
family room	la chambre pour une famille	shahñbr poor ewn fa-mee

194

single room	la chambre pour une personne	shahñbr poor ewn pehr-son
room number	le numéro de chambre	new-may-roh duh shahñbr
room service	le service dans les chambres	sehr-vees dahñ lay shahñbr

S

safe (for valuables)	le coffre-fort	kofr-for
is it safe?	ce n'est pas dangereux?	suh nay pa dahñ-zhuh-ruh?
salad	la salade	sa-lad
salad dressing	la vinaigrette	vee-neh-gret
salesman/woman	le vendeur; la vendeuse	vahñ-dur; vahñ-duhz
salt	le sel	sel
sandwich	le sandwich	sahñ-dweetsh
toasted sandwich	le croque-monsieur	krok-muh-syuh
Saturday	samedi	sam-dee
sauce	la sauce	sohs
sausage	la saucisse	so-sees
to say	dire	deer
scarf (silk)	le foulard	foo-lar
(woollen)	l'écharpe f	ay-sharp
school	l'école f	ay-kol
Scotland	l'Écosse f	ay-kos
Scottish	écossais(e)	ay-ko-seh(z)
scuba diving	la plongée sous-marine	ploñ-zhay soo-ma-reen
sea	la mer	mehr
seafood	les fruits de mer *mpl*	frwee duh mehr
season (of year)	la saison	seh-zoñ
seat (chair)	le siège	syezh
(in train)	la place	plas
(cinema, theatre)	le fauteuil	foh-tuh-yuh

second	deuxième; second(e)	duh-zyem; suh-koñ(d)
second class	seconde classe	suh-koñd klas
to see	voir	vwar
to sell	vendre	vahñdr
do you sell...?	vous vendez...?	voo vahñ-day...?
to send	envoyer	ahñ-vwa-yay
September	septembre	sep-tahñbr
service	le service	sehr-vees
is service included?	le service est compris?	luh sehr-vess ay koñ-pree?
shampoo	le shampooing	shahñ-pwañ
shaver	le rasoir électrique	ra-zwar ay-lek-treek
she	elle	el
sheet (for bed)	le drap	dra
shirt	la chemise	shuh-meez
shoe	la chaussure	shoh-sewr
shop	le magasin	ma-ga-zañ
to shop	faire du shopping	fehr dew sho-peeng
shop assistant	le vendeur; la vendeuse	vahñ-dur; vahñ-duhz
shopping centre	le centre commercial	sahñtr ko-mehr-syal
short	court(e)	koor(t)
shorts	le short	short
shoulder	l'épaule f	ay-pohl
show	le spectacle	spek-takl
shower (wash)	la douche	doosh
to have/take a shower	prendre une douche	prahñdr ewn doosh
shower gel	le gel douche	zhel doosh
sick (ill)	malade	ma-lad
I feel sick	j'ai envie de vomir	zhay ahñ-vee duh vo-meer
sign (notice)	le panneau	pa-noh
silk	la soie	swa
silver	l'argent m	ar-zhahñ

similar (to)	semblable (à)	sahñ-blabl (a)
since	depuis	duh-pwee
single (unmarried)	célibataire	say-lee-ba-tehr
(bed, room)	pour une personne	poor ewn pehr-son
single ticket	l'aller simple m	a-lay sañpl
sir	Monsieur	muh-syuh
sister	la sœur	sur
size (clothes)	la taille	ta-yuh
(shoe)	la pointure	pwañ-tewr
ski	le ski	skee
ski lift	le remonte-pente	ruh-moñt pahñt
ski pass	le forfait	for-feh
to ski	faire du ski	fehr dew skee
skin	la peau	poh
skirt	la jupe	zhewp
to sleep	dormir	dor-meer
slice (bread, salami, etc.)	la tranche	trahñsh
(cake, tart, etc.)	la part	par
slow	lent(e)	lahñ(t)
slowly	lentement	lahñ-tuh-mahñ
small	petit(e)	puh-tee(t)
to smoke	fumer	few-may
I don't smoke	je ne fume pas	zhuh nuh fewm pa
can I smoke?	on peut fumer?	oñ puh few-may?
smoked	fumé(e)	few-may
snack	le casse-croûte	kas-kroot
snail	l'escargot m	es-kar-goh
snow	la neige	nezh
soap	le savon	sa-voñ
socks	les chaussettes fpl	shoh-set
soft drink	le soda	so-da
some	du/de la/des	dew/duh la/day
someone	quelqu'un	kel-kuñ
something	quelque chose	kel-kuh shohz

English – French

sometimes	quelquefois	kel-kuh fwa
son	le fils	fees
soon	bientôt	byañ-toh
as soon as possible	dès que possible	deh kuh po-seebl
sore: *to have a sore throat*	avoir mal à la gorge	a-vwar mal a la gorzh
sorry: *I'm sorry*	excusez-moi	ek-skew-say-mwa
soup	le potage; la soupe	po-tazh; soop
south	le sud	sewd
Spain	l'Espagne *f*	es-pa-nyuh
Spanish	espagnol(e)	es-pa-nyol
sparkling (wine)	mousseux(-euse)	moo-suh(z)
(water)	gazeux(-euse)	ga-zuh(z)
to speak	parler	par-lay
do you speak English?	vous parlez anglais?	voo par-lay ahñgleh?
speciality	la spécialité	spay-sya-lee-tay
speed limit	la limitation de vitesse	lee-mee-ta-syoñ duh vee-tes
to spend (money)	dépenser	day-pahñ-say
(time)	passer	pa-say
spoon	la cuiller	kwee-yehr
sport	le sport	spor
spring (season)	le printemps	prañ-tahñ
square (in town)	la place	plas
squid	le calmar	calmar
stamp	le timbre	tañbr
to start	commencer	ko-mahñ-say
station	la gare	gar
stay	le séjour	say-zhoor
enjoy your stay	bon séjour	boñ say-zhoor
to stay (remain)	rester	res-tay
(reside for while)	loger	lo-zhay
I'm staying at...	je loge à...	zhuh lozh a...
steak	le steak	stek
sterling	la livre sterling	leevr stehr-leeng

still: *still water*	l'eau plate *f*	oh plat
stolen	volé(e)	vo-lay
stomach	l'estomac *m*	es-to-ma
to have a stomach ache	avoir mal au ventre	a-vwar mal oh vahñtr
to stop	arrêter	a-reh-tay
store (shop)	le magasin	ma-ga-zañ
storey	l'étage *m*	ay-tazh
straight on	tout droit	too drwa
strawberries	les fraises *fpl*	frez
street	la rue	rew
street map	le plan des rues	plahñ day rew
strong	fort(e)	for(t)
student	l'étudiant(e)	ay-tew-dyahñ(t)
student discount	le tarif étudiant	ta-reef ay-tew-dyahñ
stung	piqué(e)	pee-kay
suede	le daim	dañ
sugar	le sucre	sewkr
sugar-free	sans sucre	sahñ sewkr
suit (man's)	le costume	kos-tewm
(woman's)	le tailleur	ta-yur
suitcase	la valise	va-leez
summer	l'été *m*	ay-tay
sun	le soleil	so-leh-yuh
to sunbathe	prendre un bain de soleil	prahñdr uñ bañ duh so-leh-yuh
sunburn	le coup de soleil	koo duh so-leh-yuh
suncream	la crème solaire	krem so-lehr
Sunday	le dimanche	dee-mahñsh
sunglasses	les lunettes de soleil *fpl*	lew-net duh so-leh-yuh
sunny: *it's sunny*	il fait beau	eel feh boh
supermarket	le supermarché	sew-pehr-mar-shay
supper (dinner)	le souper	soo-pay
supplement	le supplément	sew-play-mahñ
surname	le nom de famille	noñ duh fa-mee

sweetener	l'édulcorant *m*	ay-dewl-ko-rahñ
sweets	les bonbons *mpl*	boñ-boñ
to swim	nager	na-zhay
swimming pool	la piscine	pee-seen
swimsuit	le maillot de bain	ma-yoh duh bañ
Swiss	suisse	swees
to switch off	éteindre	ay-tañdr
to switch on	allumer	a-lew-may
Switzerland	la Suisse	swees
swollen	enflé(e)	ahñ-flay

T

table	la table	tabl
tablet	le comprimé	koñ-pree-may
table tennis	le tennis de table	teh-nees duh tabl
table wine	le vin de table	vañ duh tabl
to take	prendre	prahñdr
to talk (to)	parler (à)	par-lay (a)
tall	grand(e)	grahñ(d)
tart	la tarte	tart
to taste	goûter	goo-tay
can I taste it	je peux goûter?	zhuh puh goo-tay?
tax	l'impôt *m*	añ-poh
taxi	le taxi	tak-see
tea	le thé	tay
herbal tea	l'infusion *f*	añ-few-zyoñ
teacher	le/la professeur	pro-feh-sur
telephone	le téléphone	tay-lay-fon
telephone box	la cabine téléphonique	ka-been tay-lay-fo-neek
telephone call	le coup de téléphone	koo duh tay-lay-fon
telephone number	le numéro de téléphone	new-may-roh duh tay-lay-fon
to telephone	téléphoner	tay-lay-fo-nay
television	la télévision	tay-lay-vee-zyoñ

temperature	la température	tahñ-pay-ra-tewr
to have a temperature	avoir de la fièvre	a-vwar duh la fyevr
tennis	le tennis	te-nees
tent	la tente	tahñt
to text	envoyer un SMS à	ahñ-vwa-yay uñ nes-em-es a
I'll text you	je t'enverrai un SMS	zhuh tahñ-veh-ray uñ nes-em-es
than	que	kuh
to thank	remercier	ruh-mehr-syay
thank you	merci	mehr-see
thank you very much	merci beaucoup	mehr-see boh-koo
that	cela/ça	suh-la/sa
that one	celui-là/celle-là	suh-lwee-la/sel-la
the	le/la/l'/les	luh/la/l'/lay
theatre	le théâtre	tay-atr
their	leur(s)	lur
them	eux	uh
there	là	la
there is/are...	il y a...	eel ya...
these	ces	say
these (ones)	ceux-ci/celles-ci	suh-see/sel-see
they	ils/elles	eel/el
thing	la chose	shohz
my things	mes affaires	may za-fehr
to think	penser	pahñ-say
thirsty: I'm thirsty	j'ai soif	zhay swaf
this	ce/ceci	suh/suh-see
this one	celui-ci/celle-ci	suh-lwee-see/sel-see
those	ces	say
those (ones)	ceux-là/celles-là	suh-la/sel-la
throat	la gorge	gorzh
through	à travers	a tra-vehr
Thursday	jeudi	zhuh-dee

ticket	le billet; le ticket	bee-yeh; tee-keh
a single ticket	un aller simple	uñ na-lay sañpl
a return ticket	un aller-retour	uñ na-lay ruh-toor
ticket office	le guichet	gee-shet
tie	la cravate	kra-vat
tight (fitting)	serré(e)	seh-ray
tights	le collant	ko-lahñ
till (cash desk)	la caisse	kes
till (until)	jusqu'à	zhews-ka
till 2 o'clock	jusqu'à deux heures	zhews-ka duh zur
time (of day)	le temps; l'heure *f*	tahñ; ur
this time	cette fois	set fwa
what time is it?	quelle heure est-il?	kel ur ay-teel?
timetable	l'horaire *m*	o-rehr
tip (to waiter, etc.)	le pourboire	poor-bwar
to tip (waiter, etc.)	donner un pourboire à	do-nay uñ poor-bwar a
tired	fatigué(e)	fa-tee-gay
to	à	a
(with name of country)	en/au	ahñ/oh
to London	à Londres	a loñdr
to the airport	à l'aéroport	a la-ay-roh-por
to France	en France	ahñ frahñs
to Canada	au Canada	oh ka-na-da
toast (to eat)	le pain grillé; le toast	pañ gree-yay; tost
today	aujourd'hui	oh-zhoor-dwee
toilet	les toilettes *fpl*	twa-let
toll (motorway)	le péage	pay-azh
tomato	la tomate	to-mat
tomorrow	demain	duh-mañ
tomorrow morning	demain matin	duh-mañ ma-tañ
tonight	ce soir	se swar
too (also)	aussi	oh-see
it's too big	c'est trop grand	say troh grahñ

it's too hot	il fait trop chaud	eel feh troh shoh
it's too noisy	il y a trop de bruit	eel ya troh duh brwee
tooth	la dent	dahñ
I have toothache	j'ai mal aux dents	zhay mal oh dahñ
toothbrush	la brosse à dents	bros a dahñ
toothpaste	le dentifrice	dahñ-tee-frees
top: *the top floor*	le dernier étage	dehr-nyay ay-tazh
top (of pyjamas, bikini, etc.)	le haut	oh
(of hill, mountain)	le sommet	so-meh
on top of	sur	sewr
total (amount)	le total	to-tal
tour	l'excursion *f*	ek-skewr-syoñ
tourist	le/la touriste	too-reest
tourist (information) office	le syndicat d'initiative; l'office de/du tourisme	sañ-dee-ka dee-nee-sya-teev; o-fees duh/dew too-reesm
towel	la serviette	sehr-vyet
town	la ville	veel
town centre	le centre-ville	sahñtr-veel
town hall	la mairie	meh-ree
town plan	le plan de la ville	plahñ duh la veel
traffic	la circulation	seer-kewla-syoñ
traffic jam	l'embouteillage *m*	ahñ-boo-tay-yazh
traffic lights	le feu	fuh
train	le train	trañ
by train	en train	ahñ trañ
the next train	le prochain train	luh pro-shañ trañ
tram	le tramway	tram-way
to translate	traduire	tra-dweer
to travel	voyager	vwa-ya-zhay
travel agent's	l'agence de voyages *f*	a-zhahñs duh vwa-yazh
tree	l'arbre *m*	arbr
trip	l'excursion *f*	ek-skewr-syoñ
trolley	le chariot	sha-ryoh

to try; to try on (clothes, shoes)	essayer	eh-say-yay
Tuesday	mardi	mar-dee
tunnel	le tunnel	tew-nel
to turn off (light, etc.)	éteindre	ay-tañdr
(engine)	couper	koo-pay
to turn on (light, etc.)	allumer	a-lew-may
(engine)	mettre en marche	metr ahñ marsh
twin-bedded room	la chambre à deux lits	shahñbr a duh lee
tyre	le pneu	pnuh

U

umbrella	le parapluie	pa-ra-plwee
uncle	l'oncle m	oñkl
uncomfortable	inconfortable	añ-koñ-for-tabl
under	sous	soo
underground (train)	le métro	may-troh
to understand	comprendre	koñ-prahñdr
I don't understand	je ne comprends pas	zhuh nuh koñ-prahñ pa
do you understand?	vous comprenez?	voo koñ-pruh-nay?
unemployed	au chômage	oh shoh-mazh
United Kingdom	le Royaume-Uni	rwa-yohm ew-nee
United States	les États-Unis mpl	ay-ta-zew-nee
university	l'université f	ew-nee-vehr-see-tay
unleaded petrol	l'essence sans plomb f	eh-sahñs sahñ ploñ
upstairs	en haut	ahñ oh
urgent	urgent(e)	ewr-zhahñ(t)
us	nous	noo
useful	utile	ew-teel
usual	habituel(-elle)	a-bee-tew-el

V

vacant	libre	leebr
vacation	les vacances *fpl*	va-kahñs
valid (ticket, driving licence, etc.)	valable; valide	va-labl; va-leed
valuables	les objets de valeur *mpl*	ob-zheh duh va-lur
VAT	la TVA	tay-vay-a
vegan	végétalien(ne)	vay-zhay-ta-lyañ/lyen
vegetables	les légumes *mpl*	lay lay-gewm
vegetarian	végétarien(ne)	vay-zhay-ta-ryañ/ryen
very	très	treh
video camera	la caméscope	ka-may-skop
village	le village	vee-lazh
vinegar	le vinaigre	vee-negr
virus	le virus	vee-rews
visa	le visa	vee-za
visit	le séjour	say-zhoor
to visit	visiter	vee-zee-tay
visitor	le/la visiteur(-euse)	vee-zee-tur/tuhz
voicemail	la messagerie vocale	meh-sa-zhree vo-kal

W

to wait for	attendre	a-tahñdr
waiter/waitress	le/la serveur(-euse)	sehr-vur/vuhz
waiting room	la salle d'attente	sal da-tahñt
to wake up	se réveiller	suh ray-vay-yay
Wales	le pays de Galles	pay-yee duh gal
walk: *to go for a walk*	faire une promenade	fehr ewn prom-nad
to walk	aller à pied; marcher	a-lay a pyay; mar-shay
wall	le mur	mewr
wallet	le portefeuille	port-fuh-yuh
to want	vouloir	voo-lwar

English	French	Pronunciation
I want...	je veux...	zhuh vuh...
we want...	nous voulons...	noo voo-loñ...
warm	chaud(e)	shoh(d)
it's warm (weather)	il fait bon	eel feh boñ
it's too warm	il fait trop chaud	eel feh troh shoh
washing machine	la machine à laver	ma-sheen a la-vay
washing powder	la lessive	leh-seev
washing-up liquid	le produit pour la vaisselle	pro-dwee poor la vay-sel
watch	la montre	moñtr
to watch (look at)	regarder	ruh-gar-day
water	l'eau *f*	oh
drinking water	l'eau potable	oh po-tabl
sparkling mineral water	l'eau minérale gazeuse	oh mee-nay-ral ga-zuhz
still mineral water	l'eau minérale plate	oh mee-nay-ral plat
watermelon	la pastèque	pas-tek
way (manner)	la manière	ma-nyehr
(route)	le chemin	shuh-mañ
way in (entrance)	l'entrée *f*	añ-tray
way out (exit)	la sortie	sor-tee
we	nous	noo
to wear	porter	por-tay
weather	le temps	tañ
weather forecast	la météo	ma-ytay-oh
Wednesday	mercredi	mehr-kruh-dee
week	la semaine	suh-men
last week	la semaine dernière	la suh-men dehr-nyehr
next week	la semaine prochaine	la suh-men pro-shen
per week	par semaine	par suh-men
this week	cette semaine	set suh-men
weekend	le week-end	wee-kend
well (healthy)	en bonne santé	añ bon sahñ-tay
he's not well	il est souffrant	eel ay soo-frahñ

I'm very well	je vais très bien	zhuh veh treh byañ
well done (steak)	bien cuit(e)	byañ kwee(t)
Welsh	gallois(e)	ga-lwa(z)
west	l'ouest *m*	oo-est
wet	mouillé(e)	moo-yay
what	que; quel/quelle; quoi	kuh; kel; kwa
what is it?	qu'est-ce que c'est?	kes kuh say?
wheelchair	le fauteuil roulant	foh-tuh-yuh roo-lahñ
when	quand	kahñ
(at what time?)	à quelle heure?	a kel ur
when is it?	c'est quand?; c'est à quelle heure?	say kahñ?; say ta kel ur?
where	où	oo
where is it?	c'est où?	say oo?
where is the hotel?	où est l'hôtel?	oo ay loh-tel?
which	quel/quelle	kel
which (one)?	lequel/laquelle?	luh-kel/la-kel?
which (ones)?	lesquels/lesquelles?	lay-kel?
white	blanc (blanche)	blahñ(sh)
who	qui	kee
who is it?	qui c'est?	kee say?
whose: *whose is it?*	c'est à qui?	say ta kee?
why	pourquoi	poor-kwa
wife	la femme	fam
window	la fenêtre	fuh-netr
(shop)	la vitrine	vee-treen
wine	le vin	vañ
wine list	la carte des vins	kart day vañ
winter	l'hiver *m*	ee-vehr
with	avec	a-vek
with ice	avec des glaçons	a-vek day gla-soñ
with milk/sugar	avec du lait/sucre	a-vek dew leh/sewkr
without	sans	soñ
without ice	sans glaçons	sahñ gla-soñ

207

without milk/ sugar	sans lait/sucre	sahñ leh/sewkr
woman	la femme	fam
wool	la laine	len
word	le mot	moh
work	le travail	tra-va-yuh
to work (person)	travailler	tra-va-yay
(machine, car)	fonctionner; marcher	foñ-ksyo-nay; mar-shay
it doesn't work	ça ne marche pas	sa nuh marsh pa
to write	écrire	ay-kreer
please write it down	vous me l'écrivez, s'il vous plaît?	voo muh lay-kree-vay seel voo pleh?
wrong	faux (fausse)	foh(s)

X

| X-ray | la radio(graphie) | ra-dyoh (gra-fee) |
| to X-ray | faire une radio | fehr ewn ra-dyoh |

Y

year	l'an *m*; l'année *f*	ahñ; a-nay
this year	cette année	set a-nay
next year	l'année prochaine	la-nay pro-shen
last year	l'année dernière	la-nay dehr-nyehr
yellow	jaune	zhohn
Yellow Pages®	les Pages Jaunes *fpl*	pazh zhohn
yes	oui	wee
yes please	oui, merci	wee, mehr-see
yesterday	hier	ee-yeehr
yet: *not yet*	pas encore	pa (z)ahñ-kor
yoghurt	le yaourt	ya-oort
plain yoghurt	le yaourt nature	ya-oort na-tewr
you (familiar)	tu	tew
(polite)	vous	voo

young	jeune	zhuhn
your (familiar singular)	**ton/ta**	toñ/ta
(familiar plural)	**tes**	tay
(polite singular)	**votre**	votr
(polite plural)	**vos**	voh
youth hostel	l'auberge de jeunesse *f*	oh-behrzh duh zhuh-nes

Z

zero	le zéro	zay-roh
zip	la fermeture éclair	fehr-muh-tewr ay-klehr
zoo	le zoo	zoh

A

à	to; at
accès interdit	no entry
accident *m*	accident
accueil *m*	reception; information
acheter	to buy
addition *f*	bill
adresse *f*	address
adressez-vous à	enquire at *(office)*
aérogare *f*	terminal
aéroport *m*	airport
affaires *fpl*	business; belongings
bonne affaire	bargain
affiche *f*	poster; notice
âge *m*	age
du troisième âge	senior citizen
âgé(e)	elderly
âgé de … ans	aged … years
agence *f*	agency; branch
agence de voyages	travel agency
agence immobilière	estate agent's
agent de police	police officer
aider	to help
aimer	to enjoy; to love *(person)*
aire: *aire de jeux*	play area
aire de repos	rest area
aire de service	service area
aire de stationnement	layby
alcool *m*	alcohol; fruit brandy
algues *fpl*	seaweed
allégé(e)	low-fat
Allemagne *f*	Germany
allemand(e)	German
aller	to go
aller (simple) *m*	single ticket
aller-retour *m*	return ticket

allumé(e)	on *(light)*
allumez vos phares	switch on headlights
alpinisme *m*	mountaineering
alsacien(ne)	Alsatian
ambassade *f*	embassy
ambulance *f*	ambulance
américain(e)	American
Amérique *f*	America
ami(e) *m/f*	friend
petit(e) ami(e)	boyfriend/girlfriend
amour *m*	love
ampoule *f*	blister; light bulb
an *m*	year
Nouvel An *m*	New Year
analgésique *m*	painkiller
ancien(ne)	old; former
angine *f*	tonsillitis
Anglais(e) *m/f*	Englishman/woman
anglais *m*	English *(language)*
anglais(e)	English
Angleterre *f*	England
animal *m*	animal
animal domestique	pet
année *f*	year; vintage
anniversaire *m*	anniversary; birthday
annonce *f*	advertisement
annulation *f*	cancellation
anti-insecte *m*	insect repellent
antibiotique *m*	antibiotic
antihistaminique *m*	antihistamine
antimoustique *m*	mosquito repellent
août	August
appareil *m*	appliance; camera
appareil acoustique	hearing aid
appareil photo	camera
appeler	to call *(speak, phone)*
appeler en PCV	to reverse the charges

appuyer	to press
après	after
après-midi *m/f*	afternoon
arbre *m*	tree
argent *m*	money; silver
argent liquide	cash
arrêt *m*	stop
arrêt d'autobus	bus stop
arrêter	to arrest; to stop
arrêter le moteur	to turn off the engine
arrêtez!	stop!
arrivées *fpl*	arrivals
arriver	to arrive; to happen
arrondissement *m*	district
article *m*	item; article
articles de toilette	toiletries
ascenseur *m*	lift
assez	enough; quite *(rather)*
assiette *f*	plate
assurance *f*	insurance
assuré(e)	insured
assurer	to assure; to insure
asthme *m*	asthma
atelier *m*	workshop; artist's studio
attacher	to fasten *(seatbelt)*
attendre	to wait (for)
attention!	look out!
faire attention	to be careful
au lieu de	instead of
au revoir	goodbye
auberge *f*	inn
auberge de jeunesse	youth hostel
aujourd'hui	today
aussi	also
autobus *m*	bus
automne *m*	autumn
autoroute *f*	motorway

autre	other
autres directions	other routes
avance: *à l'avance*	in advance
avant	before
avec	with
avion *m*	aeroplane
avis *m*	notice; warning
avoir	to have
avril	April

B

bagages *mpl*	luggage
bagages à main	hand luggage
baie *f*	bay *(along coast)*
baignade interdite	no bathing/swimming
bain *m*	bath *(act of bathing)*
bal *m*	ball; dance
balade *f*	walk; drive; trek
balcon *m*	circle *(theatre)*; balcony
ball-trap *m*	clay pigeon shooting
balle *f*	ball *(small, e.g. golf, tennis)*
ballon *m*	balloon; ball *(large)*; brandy or large wine glass
banane *f*	banana; bumbag
banc *m*	seat; bench
banlieue *f*	suburbs
banque *f*	bank
bar *m*	bar
barbe *f*	beard
barbe à papa *f*	candy floss
barque *f*	rowing boat
barrage routier	road block
bas *m*	bottom *(of page, etc.)*; stocking
en bas	below; downstairs
bas(se)	low
bateau *m*	boat; ship
bâtiment *m*	building

bâton (de ski) *m*	ski pole
beau (belle)	lovely; handsome; beautiful; nice *(enjoyable)*
beaucoup (de)	much/many; a lot of
bébé *m*	baby
belge	Belgian
Belgique *f*	Belgium
besoin: *avoir besoin de*	to need
bibliothèque *f*	library
bien	well; right; good
bien cuit(e)	well done *(steak, etc.)*
bientôt	soon; shortly
bienvenu(e)	welcome!
bière *f*	beer
bière (à la) pression	draught beer
bière blonde	lager
bière brune	bitter
bijouterie *f*	jeweller's; jewellery
billet *m*	note; ticket
billet aller-retour	return ticket
billet d'avion	plane ticket
billet de banque	banknote
billet simple	one-way ticket
bio(logique)	organic
blanc (blanche)	white; blank
blessé(e)	injured
bleu *m*	bruise
bleu(e)	blue; very rare *(steak, etc.)*
boire	to drink
bois *m*	wood
boisson *f*	drink
boisson non alcoolisée	soft drink
boîte *f*	can; box
boîte à lettres	post box
boîte de nuit	night club
bol *m*	bowl *(for soup, etc.)*
bon *m*	token; voucher

bon (bonne)	good; right; nice
bon marché	inexpensive
bonbon *m*	sweet
bonsoir	good evening
bord *m*	border; edge; verge
à bord	on board
au bord de la mer	at the seaside
bouche *f*	mouth
boucherie *f*	butcher's shop
bouée de sauvetage *f*	life belt
boulangerie *f*	bakery
boules *fpl*	game similar to bowls
Bourgogne *f*	Burgundy
bout *m*	end
bouteille *f*	bottle
bouton *m*	button; switch; spot
bouton de fièvre	cold sore
bras *m*	arm
brasserie *f*	café; brewery
Bretagne *f*	Brittany
breton(ne)	from Brittany
britannique	British
brocante *f*	second-hand goods; flea market
brouillard *m*	fog
brûlé(e)	burnt
brûlures d'estomac *fpl*	heartburn
brun(e)	brown; dark
bureau *m*	desk; office
bureau de change	foreign exchange office
bureau de poste	post office
bureau de renseignements	information office
bureau des objets trouvés	lost-property
bus *m*	bus
butane *m*	camping gas

C

ça	that
ça va	it's OK; I'm OK
ça va?	are you OK?
cabine *f*	beach hut; cubicle
cabine d'essayage	changing room
cadeau *m*	gift
café *m*	coffee; café
café au lait	white coffee
café crème	latte-like coffee
café noir	black coffee
caisse *f*	cash desk; case
calmant *m*	sedative
camping *m*	camping; campsite
Canada *m*	Canada
canadien(ne)	Canadian
canapé *m*	sofa; open sandwich
canapé-lit	sofa bed
canne à pêche *f*	fishing rod
canot de sauvetage *m*	lifeboat
car *m*	coach
carrefour *m*	crossroads
carte *f*	map; card; menu; pass *(bus, train)*
carte bleue	credit card
carte d'abonnement	season ticket
carte d'embarquement	boarding card/pass
carte d'identité	identity card
carte de crédit	credit card
carte des vins	wine list
carte postale	postcard
carte routière	road map
carte vermeille	senior citizen's rail pass
casque *m*	helmet
casque (à écouteurs)	headphones
cassé(e)	broken
casse-croûte *m*	snack

cause *f*	cause
caution *f*	security *(for loan)*; deposit
caution à verser	deposit required
cave *f*	cellar
ceci	this
cédez le passage	give way
ceinture de sécurité	seatbelt
cela	that
célèbre	famous
cent *m*	hundred
centre *m*	centre
centre commercial	shopping centre
centre de loisirs	leisure centre
centre équestre	riding school
centre-ville	city centre
cercle *m*	circle; ring
céréales *fpl*	cereal
cette	this; that
CFF *mpl*	Swiss Railways
chacun(e)	each
chaîne *f*	chain; channel; *(of mountains)* range
chaise *f*	chair
chaise de bébé	high chair
chambre *f*	bedroom; room
chambre d'hôtc	bed and breakfast
chambres	rooms to let *(on sign)*
champ *m*	field
champ de courses	racecourse
champignon vénéneux	toadstool
chance *f*	luck
chantier *m*	building site; roadworks
chaque	each; every
charbon de bois	charcoal
charcuterie *f*	pork butcher's; delicatessen; cooked meat
chariot *m*	trolley

chasse f	hunting; shooting
chasse gardée	private hunting
château m	castle; mansion
chaud(e)	hot
chauffage m	heating
chaussée déformée	uneven road surface
chaussée rétrécie	road narrows
chaussée verglacée	icy road
chaussette f	sock
chaussure f	shoe; boot
chef de train	train guard
chemin m	path; lane; track; way
chemin de fer	railway
chemise f	shirt
chemisier m	blouse
chèque de voyage	traveller's cheque
cher (chère)	dear; expensive
cheval m	horse
faire du cheval	to ride
cheveux mpl	hair
chez	at the house of
chez moi	at my home
choix m	range; choice; selection
chose f	thing
cimetière m	cemetery; graveyard
circuit m	round trip; circuit
circulation f	traffic
cirque m	circus
cité f	city; housing estate
clair(e)	clear; light
classe f	grade; class
clé f	key; spanner
clef f	key
client(e) m/f	client; customer
climatisation f	air-conditioning
climatisé(e)	air-conditioned

cocher	to 'tick' (on form – in fact, you must put a cross)
code postal	postcode
code secret	pin number
cœur *m*	heart
coffre-fort *m*	safe
coiffeur *m*	hairdresser; barber
coiffeuse *f*	hairdresser
coin *m*	corner
col *m*	collar; pass (in mountains)
combien	how much/many
combinaison de plongée *f*	wetsuit
comme	like
comme ça	like this; like that
commencer	to begin
comment	how
comment?	pardon?
commissariat (de police) *m*	police station
communication *f*	communication; call (on telephone)
compartiment *m*	compartment (train)
complet(-ète)	full (up)
composer	to dial (a number)
composter votre billet	validate your ticket
comprenant	including
comprimé *m*	tablet
compris(e)	included
non compris	not included
comptant *m*	cash
compte *m*	number; account
compte en banque	bank account
comptoir *m*	counter (in shop, bar, etc.)
concierge *m/f*	caretaker; janitor
concours *m*	contest; aid
conduire	to drive
confirmer	to confirm
congélateur *m*	freezer

conserver	to keep; to retain *(ticket, etc.)*
consigne *f*	deposit; left luggage
consommation *f*	drink
contenu *m*	contents
continuer	to continue
contraceptif *m*	contraceptive
contrat *m*	contract
contrat de location	lease
contravention *f*	fine *(penalty)*
contre	against; versus
contrôle *m*	check
contrôle des passeports	passport control
contrôle radar	speed check
contrôleur(-euse) *m/f*	ticket inspector
cordonnerie *f*	shoe repairer's
corps *m*	body
correspondance *f*	connection *(transport)*
Corse *f*	Corsica
costume *m*	suit *(man's)*
côte *f*	coast; hill; rib
Côte d'Azur	French Riviera
côté *m*	side
à côté de	beside; next to
coton *m*	cotton
couche (de bébé) *f*	nappy
couette *f*	duvet
couleur *f*	colour
couloir *m*	corridor; aisle
coup de soleil	sunburn
coup de téléphone	phone call
cour *f*	court; courtyard
courant *m*	power; current
courrier *m*	mail; post
courrier électronique	e-mail
cours *m*	lesson; course; rate
course *f*	race *(sport)*; errand
course hippique	horse race

court(e)	short
coût *m*	cost
couteau *m*	knife
couvert *m*	cover charge; place setting
couvert(e)	covered
couverture *f*	blanket; cover
crémerie *f*	dairy
crêperie *f*	pancake shop/restaurant
crise cardiaque	heart attack
croisement *m*	junction *(road)*
croisière *f*	cruise
croix *f*	cross
cru(e)	raw
cuiller/cuillère *f*	spoon
cuiller/cuillère à café	teaspoon
cuir *m*	leather
cuisine *f*	cooking; cuisine; kitchen
cuisine familiale	home cooking
cuisinière *f*	cook; cooker
cuit(e)	cooked
bien cuit(e)	well done *(steak, etc.)*
cyclisme *m*	cycling

D

dame *f*	lady
dames	ladies; ladies' (toilet)
danger *m*	danger
dangereux(-euse)	dangerous
dans	into; in; on
date *f*	date *(day)*
date de naissance	date of birth
de	from; of; some
débutant(e) *m/f*	beginner
décaféiné(e)	decaffeinated
décembre	December
déclaration de douane	customs declaration

décollage *m*	take-off *(plane)*
décoller	to take off *(plane)*
décrocher	to lift the receiver
dedans	inside
défectueux(-euse)	faulty
défense de...	no.../... forbidden
défense de fumer	no smoking
défense de stationner	no parking
dégustation de vins	wine tasting
dehors	outside; outdoors
déjeuner *m*	lunch
délicieux(-euse)	delicious
délit *m*	offence
deltaplane *m*	hang-glider
demain	tomorrow
demande *f*	application; request
demander	to ask (for)
démarqué(e)	reduced *(goods)*
demi(e)	half
demi-pension *f*	half board
demi-tarif *m*	half fare
demi-tour *m*	U-turn
dent *f*	tooth
dentifrice *m*	toothpaste
départ *m*	departure
département *m*	county
dépasser	to exceed; to overtake
déranger	to disturb
dernier(-ère)	last; latest
derrière	at the back; behind
dès: *dès votre arrivée*	as soon as you arrive
désolé(e)	sorry
dessous: *en dessous de*	underneath
dessus: *au-dessus de*	on top (of)
destination: *à destination de*	bound for
détourner	to divert
deux	two

deux fois	twice
les deux	both
deuxième	second
devant	in front (of)
devant *m*	front
déviation *f*	diversion
diabète *m*	diabetes
diarrhée *f*	diarrhoea
diététique: *produits diététiques*	health foods
difficile	difficult
dimanche *m*	Sunday
dîner *m*	dinner
dîner spectacle	cabaret dinner
dire	to say; to tell
direct: *train direct*	through train
directeur *m*	manager; headmaster
disparu(e)	missing *(disappeared)*
disponible	available
distributeur automatique	vending machine; cash machine
divertissements *mpl*	entertainment
docteur *m*	doctor
domicile *m*	home; address
dormir	to sleep
douane *f*	customs
douche *f*	shower
douleur *f*	pain
douloureux(-euse)	painful
doux (douce)	mild; gentle; soft; sweet
douzaine *f*	dozen
drogue *f*	drug
droit(e)	right *(not left)*; straight
à droite	on/to the right
tenez votre droite	keep to right
tout droit	straight on
dur(e)	hard; hard-boiled; tough

E

eau *f*	water
eau de Javel	bleach
eau minérale	mineral water
eau potable	drinking water
échelle de secours	fire escape
écluse *f*	lock *(in canal)*
école *f*	school
écossais(e)	Scottish
Écosse *f*	Scotland
écouter	to listen to
écran solaire	sunscreen lotion
écran total	sunblock
écrire	to write
édulcorant *m*	sweetener
embarquement *m*	boarding
emporter: *à emporter*	take-away
en	some; any; in; to; made of
en cas de	in case of
en face de	opposite
en gros	in bulk; wholesale
en panne	out of order
en retard	late
en train	by train
enceinte	pregnant
encore	still; yet; again
enfant *m/f*	child
enregistrement *m*	check-in desk
enregistrer	to record; to check in; to video
ensemble	together
entracte *m*	interval
entre	between
entrée *f*	entrance; admission; starter *(food)*
entrée gratuite	admission free
entrée interdite	no entry
entrez!	come in!

environs *mpl*	surroundings
épicerie *f*	grocer's shop
épicerie fine	delicatessen
épuisé(e)	sold out; used up
équipage *m*	crew
équitation *f*	horse-riding
erreur *f*	mistake
escalade *f*	climbing
escalator *m*	escalator
escalier *m*	stairs
escalier de secours	fire escape
Espagne *f*	Spain
espagnol *m*	Spanish *(language)*
espagnol(e)	Spanish
essayer	to try; to try on
essence *f*	petrol
essence sans plomb	unleaded petrol
estomac *m*	stomach
et	and
étage *m*	storey
États-Unis *mpl*	United States
été *m*	summer
éteindre	to turn off
éteint(e)	out *(light)*
étiquette *f*	label; tag
étranger(-ère) *m/f*	foreigner
être	to be
étroit(e)	narrow; tight
étudiant(e) *m/f*	student
européen(ne)	European
éviter	to avoid
exact(e)	right *(correct)*
excédent de bagages *m*	excess baggage
excès de vitesse *m*	speeding
exclu(e)	excluded
excursion *f*	trip; outing; excursion
excusez-moi!	excuse me!

exemplaire *m*	copy
exposition *f*	exhibition
extérieur(e)	outside
extra	top-quality; first-rate

F

fabriqué en...	made in...
face: *en face (de)*	opposite
facile	easy
facture *f*	invoice
faire	to make; to do
fait main	handmade
falaise *f*	cliff
famille *f*	family
farine *f*	flour
fatigué(e)	tired
fauteuil *m*	armchair; seat
fauteuil roulant	wheelchair
femme *f*	woman; wife
femme de chambre	chambermaid
femme de ménage	cleaner
fenêtre *f*	window
fente *f*	crack; slot
fer *m*: *fer à repasser*	iron *(for clothes)*
férié(e): *jour férié*	public holiday
ferme *f*	farmhouse; farm
fermé(e)	closed
fermer	to close/shut; to turn off;
fermer à clé	to lock
ferry *m*	car ferry
fête *f*	holiday; fête; party
fête foraine	funfair
feu *m*	fire; traffic lights
février	February
fièvre: *avoir de la fièvre*	to have a temperature

file *f*	lane; row
filet *m*	net; fillet *(of meat, fish)*
fille *f*	daughter; girl
fils *m*	son
fin *f*	end
fin(e)	thin *(material)*; fine *(delicate)*
fini(e)	finished
finir	to end; to finish
fleur *f*	flower
fleuriste *m/f*	florist
fleuve *m*	river
foire *f*	fair
fois *f*	time *(occasion)*
cette fois	this time
une fois	once
foncé(e)	dark *(colour)*
fonctionner	to work *(machine)*
fond *m*	back *(of hall, room)*; bottom
forêt *f*	forest
forfait *m*	fixed price; ski pass
forme *f*	shape; style
formulaire *m*	form *(document)*
four *m*	oven
frais (fraîche)	fresh; cool; wet *(paint)*
français *m*	French *(language)*
français(e)	French
frère *m*	brother
frigo *m*	fridge
froid(e)	cold
frontière *f*	border; boundary
fruit *m*	fruit
fumer	to smoke
fumeurs	smokers

G

gagner	to earn; to win
galerie *f*	art gallery; arcade; roof-rack
gallois(e)	Welsh
garage *m*	garage
garantie *f*	guarantee
garçon *m*	boy; waiter
gare *f*	railway station
gare routière	bus terminal
garer	to park
gasoil; gaz-oil *m*	diesel
gauche	left
à gauche	to/on the left
gazeux(-euse)	fizzy
gelé(e)	frozen
gendarme *m*	policeman *(in rural areas)*
gendarmerie *f*	police station
gilet *m*	waistcoat
gilet de sauvetage	life jacket
gîte *m*	self-catering house/flat
glace *f*	ice; ice cream; mirror
glacière *f*	cool-box *(for picnic)*
glissant(e)	slippery
gorge *f*	throat; gorge
goût *m*	flavour; taste
grand(e)	great; high *(speed, number)*; big; tall
grand-mère *f*	grandmother
grand-père *m*	grandfather
Grande-Bretagne *f*	Great Britain
gras(se)	fat; greasy
gratis, gratuit(e)	free (of charge)
grave	serious
grippe *f*	flu
gris(e)	grey
gros(se)	big; large; fat

grotte *f*	cave
guerre *f*	war
guichet *m*	ticket office; counter
guide *m*	guide; guidebook
guide de conversation	phrase book

H

habiter	to live (in)
halles *fpl*	covered food market
handicapé(e)	disabled *(person)*
haut *m*	top *(of ladder, bikini)*
en haut	upstairs
haut(e)	high; tall
hauteur *f*	height
hébergement *m*	lodging
herbe *f*	grass
heure *f*	hour; time of day
heure de pointe	rush hour
hier	yesterday
hippisme *m*	horse riding
hippodrome *m*	racecourse
hiver *m*	winter
hollandais(e)	Dutch
homme *m*	man
honoraires *mpl*	fee
hôpital *m*	hospital
horaire *m*	timetable; schedule
hors: *hors de*	out of
hors saison	off-season
hors service	out of order
hors taxe	duty-free
hôte *m*	host; guest
hôtel *m*	hotel
hôtel de ville	town hall
hôtesse *f*	stewardess, host
huile *f*	oil
hypermarché *m*	hypermarket

I
J

ici	here
il y a...	there is/are...; ago
il y a un défaut	there's a fault
il y a une semaine	a week ago
île *f*	island
immeuble *m*	building *(offices, flats)*
impasse *f*	dead end
imperméable	waterproof
incendie *m*	fire
inclus(e)	included; inclusive
indicatif *m*	dialling code
indigestion *f*	indigestion
infirmerie *f*	infirmary
infirmier(-ière) *m/f*	nurse
informations *fpl*	news; information
inondation *f*	flood
instant *m*	moment
un instant!	just a minute!
institut de beauté *m*	beauty salon
interdit(e)	forbidden
intéressant(e)	interesting
intérieur: à l'intérieur	indoors
introduire	to introduce; to insert
invité(e) *m/f*	guest
irlandais(e)	Irish
Irlande *f*	Ireland
Irlande du Nord *f*	Northern Ireland
issue de secours *f*	emergency exit
itinéraire *m*	route
itinéraire touristique	scenic route

J

jamais	never
jambe *f*	leg
janvier	January

Japon *m*	Japan
jardin *m*	garden
jaune	yellow
jeton *m*	token
jeu *m*	game; set *(of tools, etc.)*; gambling
jeudi *m*	Thursday
jeune	young
joli(e)	pretty
jouer	to play *(games)*
jouet *m*	toy
jour *m*	day
jour férié	public holiday
journal *m*	newspaper
journée *f*	day *(length of time)*
juif (juive)	Jewish
juillet	July
juin	June
jumelles *fpl*	twins; binoculars
jus *m*	juice
jus d'orange	orange juice
jus de fruit	fruit juice
jusqu'à/au/aux	until; till

K

kas(c)her	kosher
kilométrage illimité	unlimited mileage
kilomètre *m*	kilometre
kiosque *m*	kiosk; newsstand
klaxonner	to sound one's horn

L

là	there
lac *m*	lake
laine *f*	wool
laissez en blanc	leave blank

lait *m*	milk
lait cru	unpasteurised milk
lait démaquillant	make-up remover
lait demi-écrémé	semi-skimmed milk
lait écrémé	skimmed milk
lait entier	full-cream milk
lait longue conservation	long-life milk
lait maternisé	baby milk; formula
lait solaire	suntan lotion
lames de rasoir *fpl*	razor blades
langue *f*	tongue; language
lavable	washable
lavage *m*	washing
lave-linge *m*	washing machine
laver	to wash
se laver	to wash (oneself)
laverie automatique *f*	launderette
leçon *f*	lesson
légume *m*	vegetable
lent(e)	slow
lentement	slowly
lentille *f*	lentil; lens *(of glasses)*
lentille de contact	contact lens
lessive *f*	soap powder; washing
lettre *f*	letter
leur(s)	their
lèvre *f*	lip
librairie *f*	bookshop
libre	free; vacant
libre-service *m*	self-service
lieu *m*	place *(location)*
ligne *f*	line; service; route
limitation de vitesse *f*	speed limit
lin *m*	linen *(cloth)*
linge *m*	linen *(bed, table)*; laundry
lingettes *fpl*	baby wipes
liste *f*	list

lit *m*	bed
livre *f*	pound
livre *m*	book
location *f*	hiring (out); letting
logement *m*	accommodation
loi *f*	law
loin	far
Londres	London
long(ue)	long
le long de	along
longtemps	for a long time
louer	to let; to hire; to rent
à louer	for hire/to rent
lourd(e)	heavy
lumière *f*	light
lundi *m*	Monday
lune de miel *f*	honeymoon
lunettes *fpl*	glasses
lunettes de soleil	sunglasses
lunettes protectrices/ de protection	goggles

M

M	sign for the Paris metro
machine à laver *f*	washing machine
magasin *m*	shop
grand magasin	department store
mai	May
maillot de bain *m*	swimsuit
main *f*	hand
maintenant	now
mairie *f*	town hall
maison *f*	house; home
maison de campagne	villa
mal	badly
mal *m*	harm; pain
mal de dents	toothache

233

mal de mer	seasickness
mal de tête	headache
faire du mal à quelqu'un	to harm someone
malade	ill; sick
malade *m/f*	sick person; patient
maladie *f*	disease
Manche *f*	the Channel
manger	to eat
marchand *m*	dealer; merchant
marché *m*	market
marché aux puces	flea market
marcher	to walk; to work *(machine, car)*
en marche	on *(machine)*
mardi *m*	Tuesday
mardi gras	Shrove Tuesday
marée *f*	tide
marée basse	low tide
marée haute	high tide
mari *m*	husband
marié(e)	married
marionnette *f*	puppet
marron	brown
mars	March
matelas *m*	mattress
matériel *m*	equipment; kit
matin *m*	morning
mécanicien *m*	mechanic
médecin *m*	doctor
médicament *m*	medicine; drug; medication
Méditerranée *f*	Mediterranean Sea
meilleur(e)	best; better
mél *m*	e-mail
membre *m*	member *(of club, etc.)*
même	same
méningite *f*	meningitis
menu *m*	set menu
mer *f*	sea

merci	thank you
mercredi *m*	Wednesday
mère *f*	mother
message *m*	message
messe *f*	Mass *(church)*
messieurs *mpl*	men; gentlemen; gents' (toilet)
mesure *f*	measurement
météo *f*	weather forecast
métier *m*	trade; occupation
métro *m*	underground
mettre en marche	to turn on
meublé(e)	furnished
meubles *mpl*	furniture
midi *m*	midday; noon
Midi *m*	the south of France
mieux	better; best
mille	thousand
millimètre *m*	millimetre
mineur(e)	under age; minor
minuit *m*	midnight
minute *f*	minute
miroir *m*	mirror
mistral *m*	strong cold dry wind *(South of France)*
mixte	mixed
mode d'emploi *m*	instructions for use
moins	less; minus
moins (de)	less (than)
moins cher	cheaper
mois *m*	month
moitié *f*	half
à moitié prix	half-price
mon/ma/mes	my
monde *m*	world
moniteur(-trice)	instructor; coach
monnaie *f*	currency; change
monsieur *m*	gentleman

Monsieur m	Mr; Sir
montagne f	mountain
monter à cheval	to go horse-riding
morceau m	piece; bit; cut *(of meat)*
morsure f	bite
mot m	word; note *(letter)*
mot de passe	password
moteur m	engine; motor
moto f	motorbike
mouchoir m	handkerchief
moustique m	mosquito
moyen(ne)	average
mur m	wall
mûr(e)	mature; ripe
musée m	museum
musée d'art	art gallery
Musulman(e)	Muslim

N

natation f	swimming
nature f	wildlife
naturel(le)	natural
navette f	shuttle *(bus service)*
navigation f	sailing
négatif m	negative *(photography)*
neige f	snow
nettoyage m	cleaning
nettoyage à sec	dry-cleaning
neuf (neuve)	new
névralgie f	headache
nez m	nose
Noël m	Christmas
noir(e)	black
nom m	name; noun
nom de famille	family name
nom de jeune fille	maiden name

nombre *m*	number
nombreux(-euse)	numerous
non	no; not
non alcoolisé(e)	non-alcoholic
non-fumeurs	non-smoking
nord *m*	north
normal(e)	normal; standard *(size)*
nos	our
note *f*	note; bill; memo
notre	our
nourriture *f*	food
nouveau (nouvelle)	new
de nouveau	again
novembre	November
nuageux(-euse)	cloudy
nuit *f*	night
bonne nuit	goodnight
numéro *m*	number; act; issue

O

objectif *m*	objective; lens *(of camera)*
objet *m*	object
objets de valeur	valuable items
objets trouvés	lost property
obligatoire	compulsory
obtenir	to get; to obtain
occasion *f*	occasion; bargain
occupé(e)	busy; hired *(taxi)*; engaged
octobre	October
œil *m*	eye
office *m*	service *(church)*; office
office de/du tourisme	tourist office
offre *f*	offer
or *m*	gold
orange	orange; amber *(traffic light)*
orchestre *m*	orchestra; stalls *(in theatre)*

ordinaire	ordinary
ordinateur *m*	computer
ordonnance *f*	prescription
ordre *m*	order
à l'ordre de	payable to
oreille *f*	ear
ou	or
où	where
oublier	to forget
ouest *m*	west
oui	yes
ouvert(e)	open; on *(tap, gas, etc.)*
ouvrir	to open

P

page *f*	page
Pages Jaunes	Yellow Pages®
palais *m*	palace
panier *m*	basket
panne *f*	breakdown
panneau *m*	sign
pansement *m*	bandage
papier *m*	paper
papier cadeau	gift-wrap
papier hygiénique	toilet paper
papiers	identity papers; *(for vehicle)* documents
par exemple	for example
par jour	per day
par téléphone	by phone
parc *m*	park
parc d'attractions	funfair
parce que	because
parcmètre *m*	parking meter
pardon!	sorry!; excuse me!
parent(e) *m/f*	relative
parfait(e)	perfect

parfum *m*	perfume; flavour
parfumerie *f*	perfume shop
parking *m*	car park
parking souterrain	underground car park
parking surveillé	attended car park
parler (à)	to speak (to); to talk (to)
partie *f*	part; match *(game)*
partir	to leave; to go
à partir de	from
partout	everywhere
pas	not
passage *m*	passage
passage à niveau	level crossing
passage clouté	pedestrian crossing
passage interdit	no through way
passage souterrain	underpass
passager(-ère) *m/f*	passenger
passeport *m*	passport
passer	to pass; to spend *(time)*
se passer	to happen
passerelle *f*	gangway *(bridge)*
passe-temps *m*	hobby
pastille *f*	lozenge
patins à glace *mpl*	ice skates
patins à roulettes	roller skates
patinoire *f*	skating rink
pâtisserie *f*	cake shop; little cake
payer	to pay (for)
payé(e)	paid
payé(e) d'avance	prepaid
pays *m*	land; country
du pays	local
Pays-Bas *mpl*	Netherlands
Pays de Galles *m*	Wales
péage *m*	toll *(motorway, etc.)*
peau *f*	skin; hide *(leather)*
pêche *f*	peach; fishing

pêcher	to fish
pédalo *m*	pedal boat/pedalo
pelote *f*	ball
pelote basque	pelota *(ball game for two players)*
pendant	during
pendant que	while
pension *f*	guesthouse
pension complète	full board
pente *f*	slope
perdre	to lose
perdu(e)	lost *(object)*
père *m*	father
périmé(e)	out of date; expired
périphérique *m*	ring road
permis *m*	permit; licence
permis de chasse	hunting permit
permis de conduire	driving licence
permis de pêche	fishing permit
personne *f*	person
pétanque *f*	type of bowls
petit(e)	small; slight
petit-déjeuner	breakfast
peu	little; few
à peu près	approximately
un peu (de)	a bit (of)
phare *m*	headlight; lighthouse
pharmacie *f*	chemist's; pharmacy
pichet *m*	jug; carafe
pièce *f*	room *(in house)*; play *(theatre)*; coin
pièce d'identité	means of identification
pièce de rechange	spare part
pied *m*	foot
à pied	on foot
piéton *m*	pedestrian
pile *f*	pile; battery

pilule *f*	(contraceptive) pill
piquet *m*	peg *(for tent)*
piqûre *f*	insect bite; injection; sting
piscine *f*	swimming pool
piste *f*	ski-run; runway
piste de luge	toboggan run
piste pour débutants	nursery slope
placard *m*	cupboard
place *f*	square *(in town)*; seat; space *(room)*
plage *f*	beach
plainte *f*	complaint
plaisir *m*	enjoyment; pleasure
plaît: s'il vous/te plaît	please
plan *m*	map *(of town)*
plan de la ville	street map
planche *f*	plank
planche à repasser	ironing board
planche à voile	sailboard(ing); windsurf board; windsurfing
planche de surf	surfboard
plat *m*	dish; course *(of meal)*; main course
plat principal	main course
plein(e) (de)	full (of)
le plein!	fill it up! *(car)*
plein tarif	peak rate; full fare
pleuvoir	to rain
il pleut	it's raining
plonger	to dive
pluie *f*	rain
plus	more; most
plus grand(e) (que)	bigger (than)
plus tard	later
pneu *m*	tyre
pneu crevé	burst tyre
pneu dégonflé	flat tyre

poche *f*	pocket
poêle *f*	frying pan
poids *m*	weight
poids lourd	heavy goods vehicle
point *m*	place; point; stitch; dot
pointure *f*	size *(of shoes)*
poison *m*	poison
poissonnerie *f*	fishmonger's shop
police *f*	policy *(insurance)*; police
pompiers *mpl*	fire brigade
pont *m*	bridge; deck *(of ship)*
port *m*	harbour; port
portable *m*	mobile phone; laptop
porte *f*	door; gate
portefeuille *m*	wallet
porter	to wear; to carry
porte-clefs *m*	keyring
porte-monnaie *m*	purse
poste *f*	post; post office
poste de contrôle	checkpoint
poste de secours	first-aid post
poster	to post
potable	drinkable; drinking *(water)*
poterie *f*	pottery
poudre *f*	powder
pour	for
pourboire *m*	tip
pourquoi	why
pousser	to push
poussette *f*	push chair
premier(-ière)	first
premiers secours	first aid
prendre	to take; to get; to catch
prénom *m*	first name
près de	near (to)
préservatif *m*	condom
pressing *m*	dry cleaner's

prêt(e)	ready
prêt-à-porter m	off-the-peg clothes
prévision f	forecast
prière de...	please...
principal(e)	main
printemps m	spring
priorité f	right of way
priorité à droite	give way to traffic from right
privé(e)	private
prix m	price; prize
à prix réduit	cut-price
prix d'entrée	admission fee
problème m	problem
prochain(e)	next
proche	close (near)
produits mpl	produce; product
profond(e)	deep
promotionnel(le)	on offer
propriétaire m/f	owner
propriété f	property
provisoire	temporary
public m	audience
pull(over) m	sweater
PV m	parking ticket

Q

quai m	platform
quand	when
quart m	quarter
quartier m	neighbourhood; district
que	that; than; whom; what
qu'est-ce que c'est?	what is it?
quel(le)	which; what
quelque	some
quelque chose	something
queue: faire la queue	to queue (up)
qui	who; which

R

rabais *m*	reduction
radio(graphie) *f*	X-ray
rafraîchissements *mpl*	refreshments
rage *f*	rabies
ralentir	to slow down
randonnée *f*	hike
randonnée à cheval	pony-trekking
rapide *m*	express train
rappel *m*	reminder *(on signs)*
raquette *f*	racket; bat; snowshoe
rasoir *m*	razor
RATP *f*	Paris transport authority
RC	ground floor
récepteur *m*	receiver *(of phone)*
réception *f*	reception; check-in
recette *f*	recipe
réchaud de camping *m*	camping stove
réclamation *f*	complaint
reçu *m*	receipt
réduction *f*	reduction; discount; concession
régime *m*	diet
région *f*	region
reine *f*	queen
relais routier *m*	roadside restaurant
remède *m*	remedy
remplir	to fill (up); to fill in/out
rencontrer	to meet
rendez-vous *m*	date; appointment
renseignements *mpl*	information
réparations *fpl*	repairs
repas *m*	meal
repasser	to iron
répondre (à)	to reply; to answer
réponse *f*	answer; reply
représentation *f*	performance

requis(e)	required
RER m	high-speed Paris commuter train
réservation f	reservation; booking
réservé(e)	reserved
réserve naturelle f	nature reserve
restoroute m	roadside or motorway restaurant
retard m	delay
retour m	return
retourner	to go back
retrait m	withdrawal; collection
retrait d'espèces	cash withdrawal
retraité(e)	retired; old-age pensioner
réveil m	alarm clock
rez-de-chaussée m	ground floor
rhume m	cold *(illness)*
rhume des foins	hay fever
rien	nothing
rien à déclarer	nothing to declare
rivière f	river
RN f	trunk road
roi m	king
roman(e)	Romanesque
rond(e)	round
rond-point m	roundabout
rose	pink
rose f	rose
rôtisserie f	steakhouse; roast meat counter
roue f	wheel
roue de secours	spare wheel
rouge	red
rougeur f	rash *(skin)*
route f	road; route
route barrée	road closed
Royaume-Uni m	United Kingdom

rue *f*	street
rue sans issue	no through road
ruelle *f*	lane; alley
russe	Russian

S

sable *m*	sand
sables mouvants	quicksand
sac *m*	sack; bag
sac à dos	backpack
sac à main	handbag
sac de couchage	sleeping bag
saison *f*	season
basse saison	low season
de saison	in season
haute saison	high season
salle *f*	lounge *(airport)*; hall; ward *(hospital)*
salle à manger	dining room
salle d'attente	waiting room
salle de bains	bathroom
salon *m*	sitting room; lounge
samedi *m*	Saturday
SAMU *m*	emergency services
sang *m*	blood
sans	without
sans alcool	alcohol-free
sans issue	no through road
santé *f*	health
sapeurs-pompiers *mpl*	fire brigade
sauf	except *(for)*
savoir	to know *(be aware of)*
savoir faire quelque chose	to know how to do sth
savon *m*	soap
scène *f*	stage
sec (sèche)	dry; dried *(fruit, beans, etc.)*
sèche-cheveux *m*	hairdryer

second(e)	second *(in sequence)*
seconde *f*	second *(in time)*
secours *m*	help
au secours!	help!
sécurité *f*	security; safety
séjour *m*	stay; visit
sel *m*	salt
self *m*	self-service restaurant
semaine *f*	week
sens *m*	meaning; direction
sens interdit	no entry
sens unique	one-way street
septembre	September
seringue *f*	syringe
serrure *f*	lock
servez-vous	help yourself
service *m*	service; service charge; favour
service compris	service included
service d'urgences	emergency services
serviette *f*	towel; briefcase
serviette hygiénique	sanitary towel
seulement	only
sexe *m*	sex
shampooing *m*	shampoo
short *m*	shorts
si	if; yes *(to negative question)*
siècle *m*	century
siège *m*	seat; head office
signer	to sign
situé(e)	located
ski *m*	ski; skiing
ski de piste	downhill skiing
ski de randonnée/fond	cross-country skiing
ski nautique	water-skiing
SNCB *f*	Belgian Railways
SNCF *f*	French Railways
société *f*	company; society

sœur f	sister
soie f	silk
soif f	thirst
avoir soif	to be thirsty
soin m	care
soins du visage	facial
soir m	evening
soirée f	evening; party
soldes mpl	sales
soleil m	sun; sunshine
somnifère m	sleeping pill
sorte f	kind (sort, type)
sortie f	exit
sortie de secours	emergency exit
sortie interdite	no exit
sortir	to go out (leave)
souper m	supper
sourd(e)	deaf
sous	underneath; under
sous-sol m	basement
sous-titres mpl	subtitles
souterrain(e)	underground
souvent	often
sparadrap m	sticking plaster
spectacle m	show (in theatre); entertainment
sport m	sport
sports nautiques	water-sports
stade m	stadium
stage m	course
station f	station (metro); resort
station balnéaire	seaside resort
station de taxis	taxi rank
station-service	service station
station thermale	spa
stationnement m	parking
sud m	south

suisse	Swiss
Suisse *f*	Switzerland
suivre	to follow
supermarché *m*	supermarket
supplément *m*	extra charge
supplémentaire	extra
sur	on; onto; on top of; upon
sur place	on the spot
sûr	safe; sure
surf *m*	surfing
faire du surf	to surf
surf des neiges	snowboarding
syndicat d'initiative *m*	tourist office

T

tabac *m*	tobacco; tobacconist's
table *f*	table
tableau *m*	painting; picture; board
taille *f*	size *(of clothes)*; waist
taille unique	one size
grande taille	extra large *(clothes)*
tard	late
tarif *m*	price-list; rate; tariff
tasse *f*	cup; mug
taux *m*	rate
taux de change	exchange rate
taxe *f*	duty; tax *(on goods)*
taxi *m*	cab *(taxi)*
télé *f*	TV
télécabine *f*	gondola lift
télécarte *f*	phonecard
téléphérique *m*	cable-car
téléphone *m*	telephone
(téléphone) portable	mobile phone
téléphoner (à)	to phone
télésiège *m*	chair-lift
télévision *f*	television

temps *m*	weather; time
tenir	to hold; to keep
tension *f*	voltage; blood pressure
tente *f*	tent
tenue *f*	clothes; dress
tenue de soirée	evening dress
terrain *m*	ground; land; pitch; course
terrasse *f*	terrace
tête *f*	head
TGV *m*	high-speed train
thé *m*	tea
thé au lait	tea with milk
thé nature	black tea
théâtre *m*	theatre
ticket *m*	ticket *(bus, cinema, museum)*
ticket de caisse	receipt
timbre *m*	stamp
tirer	to pull
tirez	pull
toilettes *fpl*	toilet(s); washroom
tonalité *f*	dialling tone
tôt	early
total *m*	total *(amount)*
toucher	to touch
toujours	always; still; forever
tour *f*	tower
tour *m*	trip; walk; ride
tourisme *m*	sightseeing
tourner	to turn
tous	everyone; all
tous les jours	daily
tousser	to cough
tout	everything
tout/toute/toutes/tous	all
tout à l'heure	in a while
tout compris	all inclusive
tout de suite	straight away

tout droit	straight ahead
tout le monde	everyone
toutes directions	all routes
toux *f*	cough
tradition *f*	custom (tradition)
traduction *f*	translation
train *m*	train
tranche *f*	slice
tranquille	quiet (place)
travail *m*	work
travailler	to work (person)
travaux *mpl*	road works; alterations (building)
travers: à travers	through
traverser	to cross (road, sea)
tremplin de ski *m*	ski jump
très	very; much
trop	too; too much
trottoir *m*	pavement; sidewalk
trou *m*	hole
trousse de premiers secours *f*	first aid kit
TVA *f*	VAT
typique	typical

U

UE *f*	EU
un(e)	one; a; an
l'un ou l'autre	either one
université *f*	university
urgence *f*	urgency; emergency
urgences	accident and emergency department
usine *f*	factory
utiliser	to use

vacances *fpl*	holiday(s)
en vacances	on holiday
grandes vacances	summer holiday(s)
vaccin *m*	vaccination
vache *f*	cow
valable	valid *(ticket, licence, etc.)*
valeur *f*	value
valise *f*	suitcase
vallée *f*	valley
valoir	to be worth
ça vaut...	it's worth...
végétal(e)	vegetable
végétalien(ne)	vegan
végétarien(ne)	vegetarian
véhicule *m*	vehicle
véhicules lents	slow vehicles
vélo *m*	bike
vendre	to sell
à vendre	for sale
vendredi *m*	Friday
vénéneux(-euse)	poisonous
venir	to come
vent *m*	wind
vente *f*	sale
verglas *m*	black ice
verre *m*	glass
verres de contact	contact lenses
vers	toward(s); about
vestiaire *m*	cloakroom
vêtements *mpl*	clothes
vétérinaire *m/f*	vet
veuillez...	please...
via	by *(via)*
viande *f*	meat
vieux (vieille)	old

vigne *f*	vine; vineyard
vignoble *m*	vineyard
village *m*	village
ville *f*	town; city
vin *m*	wine
virage *m*	bend; corner
visage *m*	face
visite *f*	visit; consultation *(of doctor)*
visite guidée	guided tour
visiteur(-euse) *m/f*	visitor
vite	quickly; fast
vitesse *f*	gear *(of car)*; speed
vitesse limitée à...	speed limit...
vivre	to live
voici	here is/are
voie *f*	lane (of road); line; track
voilà	there you are
voile *f*	sail; sailing
voilier *m*	sailing boat
voir	to see
voisin(e) *m/f*	neighbour
voiture *f*	car; coach *(of train)*
vol *m*	flight; theft
vol intérieur	domestic flight
volonté: à volonté	as much as you like
voyageur(-euse) *m/f*	traveller
VTT *m*	mountain bike
vue *f*	view; sight

W

W-C *mpl*	toilet(s); washroom
wagon-couchettes *m*	sleeping car
wagon-restaurant *m*	dining car

Y

yaourt *m*   yoghurt
yaourt nature   plain yoghurt
yeux *mpl*   eyes
youyou *m*   dinghy

Z

zéro *m*   zero
zone *f*   zone
zone piétonne   pedestrian area
zoo *m*   zoo